Routledge Revivals

What The League Of Nations Is

Originally published in 1925, written by someone who was associated with the work of the League of Nations from the beginning, this concise book is a clear and short account of the structure, function and tasks of the League of Nations at the start of the Twentieth Century. The necessary historical background to the political landscape at the end of World War 1 is provided and the early chapters deal with The Peace Conference and the Covenant as well as the signing of the Treaty. Later chapters examine the role of the International Labour Organization, the Court of International Justice, The Geneva Protocol, economic and financial organization and the restructuring of Europe.

What The League Of Nations Is

H. Wilson Harris

Routledge
Taylor & Francis Group

First published in 1925 by George Allen & Unwin Ltd

This edition first published in 2024 by Routledge
4 Park Square, Milton Park, Abingdon, Oxon, OX14 4RN
and by Routledge
605 Third Avenue, New York, NY 10158.

Routledge is an imprint of the Taylor & Francis Group, an informa business

© 1925 H. Wilson Harris

The right of H. Wilson Harris to be identified as the author of this work has been
asserted by him in accordance with sections 77 and 78 of the Copyright, Designs and
Patents Act 1988.

ISBN 13: 978-1-032-94852-2 (hbk)
ISBN 13: 978-1-003-58207-6 (ebk)
ISBN 13: 978-1-032-94867-6 (pbk)
Book DOI 10.4324/9781003582076

WHAT THE LEAGUE
OF NATIONS IS

BY

H. WILSON HARRIS, M.A.

LONDON: GEORGE ALLEN & UNWIN LTD.
RUSKIN HOUSE, 40 MUSEUM STREET, W.C.1

First published in 1925

Printed in Great Britain

FOREWORD

IF any excuse is required for the appearance of this modest volume it is to be found in the fact that, so far as I am aware, there exists no book which tells in small compass, and at a reasonable figure, the plain story of how the League of Nations was created, and what it has done and is doing. I believe such a statement is needed, and I have tried to provide it.

H. WILSON HARRIS.

LONDON,
February 1925.

CONTENTS

WHAT THE LEAGUE OF NATIONS IS

CHAPTER I

HOW THE LEAGUE BEGAN

The Peace Conference and the Covenant—How the ground had been prepared—The framing of the Covenant—The signing of the Treaty—The first Council Meeting.

On a close afternoon at the end of April 1919 the Banqueting Hall of the Quai d'Orsay, in Paris, was crowded with Peace Conference delegates and officials. A Plenary Session was in progress. M. Clemenceau, in the chair, leaned forward on the table, his hands in their inevitable grey gloves clasped in front of him. On his right was President Wilson, on his left Mr. Lloyd George. Round the horse-shoe tables that filled the room the fifty or sixty other plenipotentiaries were ranged. The business before the Conference was the adoption of the Covenant of the League of Nations and the appointment of a Council and Secretary-General for the League.

The speeches, for the most part admirable but unnecessary, droned on till the hands of the clock pointed to five. The orator then on his feet subsided. M. Clemenceau suddenly rose. "Does anyone else desire to speak ? " he demanded, continuing without perceptible pause, " The resolution has been moved and seconded. Is there any opposition ? The resolution is carried." So, in a manner did the League of Nations spring to birth.

But in a manner only, for till the Peace Treaty that embodied the Covenant was ratified the League could have no active existence. It was not till January 1920 that it entered on the plenitude of its power. In that month another scene, memorable in the history of the League, was enacted in an adjoining chamber of the same Ministère des Affaires Étrangères at Paris, when, at a minute or two after 10.30 on the 16th, M. Léon Bourgeois, President of the French Senate, rising from his seat at the head of an oval table underneath the famous clock in the Salle de l'Horloge, pronounced a dozen words that will stand on record as historic : " Messieurs, la séance du Conseil de la Société des Nations est ouverte."

Round the table were grouped a Prime Minister (M. Venizelos), two Foreign Secretaries (Lord Curzon and M. Paul Hymans), an Italian Senator, three Ambassadors, and the Secretary-General of the League (Sir Eric Drummond). Mr. Lloyd George had a seat among the spectators, and before the sitting was far advanced a commanding, black-spectacled figure had risen by request from his place in the body of the hall and moved to the table, that Lord Grey of Fallodon might receive thus publicly and in due form the thanks of the Council for his part in preparing the soil for the growth of the ideals of the League of Nations.

The preparation of the soil had, in fact, been going forward long before the lifetime of Lord Grey, or the oldest man present with him in the Salle de l'Horloge on that day, for the League as a political conception was an inevitable outcome of the developing contacts between nations induced by the swiftly increasing efficiency of physical communications through the whole, and particularly the latter half, of the nineteenth century. If the war brought a momentary setback to that impulse to closer co-operation between nations, it gave it in reality a new impetus by displaying before the world the two inevitable alternatives, on the one hand still closer co-operation in the interests of peace, and on the other drift, devastation and despair.

As early as 1914 definite plans for the construction of a League of Nations were attracting some public attention in Great Britain, an article by the late Mr. Aneurin Williams, M.P., in the *Contemporary Review* of November, being one of the first landmarks in the movement. About the same time, Mr. Asquith and Sir Edward Grey were advocating the formation of a League of Nations after the war, and in 1916, at the instance of Lord Robert Cecil, a strong Foreign Office Committee, under the chairmanship of Lord Phillimore, was appointed to work out a plan. Simultaneously public men in other countries, notably President Wilson and Ex-President Taft in America, M. Léon Bourgeois in France and (a little later) General Smuts in South Africa, were proceeding independently along the same lines. The result was that when the Peace Conference met at Paris at the beginning of 1919 the delegates were already committed to the creation of the League, for the last of President Wilson's famous Fourteen Points, on the basis of which the Allies had offered, and Germany had accepted, the Armistice, stipulated that " a general association of nations must be formed under specific covenants for the purpose of affording mutual guarantees of political independence and territorial integrity to great and small States alike."

In point of fact the framing of the League of Nations Covenant was the first piece of work put through by the Peace Conference. The task was entrusted to a special commission, appointed at one of the earliest sittings of the Conference. President Wilson was its chairman, and among its members were some of the most prominent men then in Paris. Lord Robert Cecil was one of them, so was General Smuts, so were M. Venizelos of Greece, M. Léon Bourgeois of France, Signor Orlando of Italy, M. Paul Hymans of Belgium, Baron Makino of Japan, Dr. Wellington Koo of China. Four delegations, the British, the American, the French and the Italian, had worked out schemes of their own. The two latter were set aside and the Commission took as its basis a composite draft embodying the chief features of the British and American plans. No body of men in Paris worked harder and none with greater harmony. Meetings were held late at night, because most of the members were already on other committees during the day, and they were held six or seven times a week. The fabric of the Covenant, as President Wilson, influenced by his Presbyterian ancestry, insisted on calling it, took shape swiftly. On various points there were differences of opinion. That was inevitable. The British and Americans at first wanted a Council consisting only of Great Powers, but the smaller States insisted on getting places, and got them. The French wanted a League army, or failing that a League general staff, but all President Wilson and Lord Robert Cecil would agree to was a standing committee of naval and military experts to advise the Council. President Wilson wanted nothing but arbitration in the case of disputes. Lord Robert Cecil stood for a formal Court of Justice to deal with legal questions, and provision for the creation of such a Court was inserted in the Covenant.

The League Commission laid its first draft of the Covenant before the full Peace Conference in the middle of February. It was provisionally approved and published, so that the Commission could profit by criticism in the Press and elsewhere. Thirteen neutral States were invited to Paris to give their views on the plan the Allied delegates had prepared. In the light of their comments, of opinions expressed in other quarters and in particular of the representations made to President Wilson when he went back to America for a flying visit at the end of February, the first draft was reconsidered and put into final shape. At the end of April the Commission's text was adopted without the change of a comma by the full Conference, being the first part of the Treaty of Versailles to be thus formally approved by the whole body of delegates. For it had already been decided that the Covenant should form part of the Treaty, so that no State could make peace with Germany without at the same time making itself a member of the new international society designed to keep peace for the future between all nations.

At the end of June the Treaty, and as a consequence the Covenant, was signed in the Hall of Mirrors at Versailles. But a treaty is not effective till ratified by a certain agreed number of signatories, and it was another six months before the Treaty of Versailles came into force. Till that happened the League could have no actual existence. But full use was, in fact, made of the interval, for the chief official of the League, its first Secretary-General, Sir Eric Drummond, had been nominated in an Annexe to the Covenant itself, and between June 1919 and January 1920 he was able, with funds advanced by the British Government, to build up a staff in temporary offices in London, so that when the Treaty of Versailles came effectively into operation on January 10, 1920, the League machinery was already in existence, not merely on paper but in actual flesh and blood, and the preparations for the first Council meeting on January 16th were as efficient as those for the thirty-second meeting at the end of 1924. With the holding of that meeting in the Clock Room of the French Foreign Office, the League of Nations' public career was begun.

CHAPTER II

THE PURPOSE OF THE LEAGUE

Who the Members are—The Covenant analysed—Tasks outside the Covenant.

BUT to explain how the League of Nations began is by no means the same thing as explaining what the League of Nations is. The latter question can be answered partly by examining the League's actual constitution and partly by reviewing, however briefly, what it has actually done in its first five years of existence. The present chapter will be devoted to the former task, the rest of the book to the latter.

Out of the Peace Conference, as has been shown, there came the League of Nations Covenant. The Covenant, consisting of a Preamble, twenty-six Articles and two Annexes, laid down briefly what States the League was to consist of, what work it was to do, and how it was to do it. The membership question may be considered first. The theory of the League has always been that it shall include all nations, but never that it shall include them automatically. Apart from the original members, States desiring to join the League have to make definite application, fulfil certain conditions and give certain assurances. But the great majority of the States of the world did, in fact, come in as original members. They fell into two categories, the Allied Powers who signed the Covenant as part of the Treaty of Versailles, and a certain number of neutrals, specially named in an Annexe to the Covenant, who were invited to join and accepted.

There were thirty-one Allied signatories, of whom three never ratified the Treaty, and therefore never became members of the League, and thirteen neutrals. One State, China, though it never signed the Treaty of Versailles, did sign and ratify the Treaty of St. Germain with Austria, which (like the treaties with Hungary and Bulgaria) also embodies the Covenant, and entered the League that way. The total number of League members at the opening of the First Assembly in 1920 was therefore forty-two. During that Assembly six new members were admitted, and another seven at the Assemblies of 1921, 1922, 1923 and 1924, the membership of the League at the end of the Fifth Assembly being thus fifty-five.[1] The most notable

[1] Made up as follows :

Original Allied Members

Belgium	Cuba	Panama
Bolivia	France	Peru
Brazil	Greece	Poland
British Empire	Guatemala	Portugal
Canada	Haiti	Rumania
Australia	Honduras	Serb-Croat-Slovene
South Africa	Italy	State
New Zealand	Japan	Siam
India	Liberia	Czechoslovakia
China	Nicaragua	Uruguay

Original Neutral Members

Argentine Republic	Norway	Spain
Chile	Paraguay	Sweden
Colombia	Persia	Switzerland
Denmark	Salvador	Venezuela
Netherlands		

Subsequently admitted

Albania, 1920.	Latvia, 1921.
Austria, 1920.	Lithuania, 1921.
Bulgaria, 1920.	Hungary, 1922.
Costa Rica, 1920	Irish Free State, 1923.
Finland, 1920.	Abyssinia, 1923.
Luxemburg, 1920.	San Domingo, 1924.
Esthonia, 1921.	

absentees at that date were the United States, Germany, Russia, Mexico, Turkey and Egypt. The principal qualification for entry into the League is that of being a " fully self-governing State, Dominion or Colony," though one or two of the original members, notably India, could hardly have passed that test. In addition to India the four Dominions of Canada, Australia, South Africa and New Zealand came in as full members independent of Great Britain, and the Irish Free State was admitted subsequently (in 1923) on the same basis.

But the question of whom the League was to consist is hardly as important as the question of what it was to do. That is clearly enough set out in the Covenant itself, and nowhere more clearly than in the Preamble, which defines the League's objects so clearly as to be worth reproducing as it stands.

"THE HIGH CONTRACTING PARTIES

In order to promote international co-operation and to achieve international peace and security
  by the acceptance of obligations not to resort to war,
  by the prescription of open, just and honourable relations between nations,
  by the firm establishment of the understandings of international law as the actual rule of conduct among Governments, and
  by the maintenance of justice and a scrupulous respect for all treaty obligations in the dealings of organized peoples with one another,
Agree to this Covenant of the League of Nations."

As a fairly concise statement of aims the Preamble serves well enough, but something much more explicit was needed than that, and something much more explicit was provided by the twenty-six Articles that form the main body of the Covenant. Through what machinery, it may, for example, be asked, was the

League to operate ? The first seven Articles supply the answer. Through an Assembly, a Council and a permanent Secretariat, full details concerning their appointment and functions being added.[1] How are funds to be raised ? Article VI answers that question by providing for a scale of contributions to be framed. How was international peace and security (in the words of the Preamble) to be achieved ? Partly by securing an all-round reduction of national armaments, as to which Articles VIII and IX prescribe a definite procedure, and partly by providing mechanism for the peaceful settlement of all international disputes, a matter into which Articles XI and XVII enter fully,[2] while Article XVI indicates methods of dealing with States which insist on going to war in breach of their Covenant pledges.

So much for " the acceptance of obligations not to resort to war." But at least as important as that negative undertaking is the first object of all laid down in the Preamble, the promotion of international co-operation. That kind of co-operation was not unknown before the League was created. The Universal Postal Union, for example, had existed for over forty years, and a number of isolated general conventions like the Red Cross, or the agreement for the control of the drug traffic drafted at The Hague in 1912, showed that nations could work together when they chose. The Covenant was designed both to co-ordinate and to stimulate all such movements by associating all the examples of co-operation in technical matters with the great new experiment in permanent political co-operation—for this was the fundamentally new departure—set in motion at Geneva. Accordingly, Articles XXIII and XXIV of the Covenant bring

[1] See Chapter III.   [2] See Chapter VI.

under the ægis of the League all international offices already established by general treaties (subject to the consent of the signatories, the great majority of whom are of course members of the League), and in particular lays on the League special responsibility in such matters as labour conditions, the treatment of native inhabitants of subject territories, the traffic in women and children, the arms traffic, the opium and dangerous drug traffic, health, communications and transit.

This is not a completely exhaustive analysis of the Covenant. If it were, reference would have to be made to the much contested Article X, under which League members undertake to defend one another against anything like permanent occupation or annexation by another State, and to various provisions such as those for the registration and publication of all international treaties (Article XVIII), the review of treaties no longer applicable (Article XIX), and the highly important plan for the administration of non-European territories captured from Germany and Turkey under a special mandate from the League (Article XXII). No analysis of the Covenant ought in any case to be regarded as exhaustive, for the Covenant itself is not exhaustive and was never meant to be. If it were properly conceived of as rigidly limiting the sphere of activity of the League, it might justly be condemned as embodying the worst vices of a written constitution. What it does represent is the minimum advance signatory States are prepared to make in the direction of international co-operation. No one can compel any one of them to go beyond the Covenant, for there is no over-ruling of minorities by majorities at Geneva. Outside the explicit pledges embodied in the Covenant every State retains its full liberty of action. On the other hand—and this is much the most important side of the question to emphasize—States who meet in Council or Assembly at Geneva are, of course, perfectly free to take by unanimous agreement any kind of action that seems wise, whether it falls strictly within the four corners of the Covenant or not.

In point of fact it would be hard to find any Article in the Covenant to cover what is perhaps the most important work the League has yet achieved, the preparation and administration of the financial reconstruction schemes in Austria, Hungary and Greece. It is as a starting-point, and no more than a starting-point, in international co-operation that the Covenant must be regarded. That was how its actual framers at Paris in 1919 did regard it. So far, at least, they could see ahead. For the rest, the League should shape its own course as it lived and worked. So, accordingly, it is shaping it. Whether the Covenant is amended so as to enlarge the scope of the League's work, or whether the scope is simply enlarged without reference to the Covenant, matters relatively little. The Covenant was necessary, for no nation will undertake indefinite obligations, and it had to be made perfectly clear to what every Member-State was binding itself in entering the League. But for the League to regard itself as fettered by what was meant to be a charter of enlarging action would be fatal. Fortunately no signs of such a danger have appeared.

CHAPTER III

THE STRUCTURE OF THE LEAGUE

The Assembly—The Council—How the Council is chosen—
The Unanimous Vote—The Language Problem—Technical
Organizations and Advisory Committees—The Secretariat
—The League's Finance.

THE working machinery of the League is partly what
the Covenant laid down and partly what practical
experience has since dictated. The Covenant provided
for three main wheels in the mechanism, an Assembly,
a Council and a permanent Secretariat, and indicated
how the Assembly and the Council should be constituted and the Secretariat appointed. Practical
experience has shown that while these three bodies
are, and must be, the chief instruments of the League's
activity, a field of work so wide and varied makes
expert advice on many questions essential, and there
has, therefore, been built up a series of technical
committees (on financial and economic problems,
transit questions, health, and so forth), each of them
served by a corresponding technical section of the
Secretariat, to advise the Council on particular questions. Since the advice is practically always taken,
the committees tend to have in effect the status of
autonomous bodies reaching what are in practice final
conclusions on the questions they handle.

The vital difference between the Assembly and the
Council is that the former consists of representatives

of all States members of the League, and the latter of representatives, originally of only eight, and later of ten, States. According to Article III of the Covenant each State may send not more than three representatives to the Assembly, though the whole delegation casts only a single vote. To put the matter in another way, every State has one vote at the Assembly, but it can send as many as three representatives to speak and to sit on committees. As a matter of fact, most States send more than three, for in addition to the full delegates, substitute-delegates, with almost the same powers, can be sent in unlimited numbers. Since the Assembly, which meets at Geneva on the first Monday in every September and sits for about a month, can only get through its business by devolving it on to six large committees, most countries endeavour to send to Geneva three substitute-delegates in addition to the three delegates, so as to have a separate representative on each of the committees. The British delegation, for example, to a League Assembly, usually consists of three full delegates, three or four substitute-delegates and a certain number of expert advisers from the various Government Departments in Whitehall, together with private secretaries, typists and one or two messengers, the total contingent, including all grades, numbering perhaps twenty-five to thirty persons.

Every country appoints its delegates in its own way. In practically every case the Prime Minister nominates them, and it is understood that while the speech of a delegate from an Assembly platform need not be held to commit the Government represented to the views expressed, the vote given by a delegation on any question is given on behalf of its Government. There is, therefore, room for a certain play of individual opinion within a delegation—Mr. George Barnes, for example, at the First Assembly expressed views on Russia and Poland with which his two colleagues in the British delegation would certainly not have been prepared to identify themselves—but at the same time the essential principle that the Assembly is a body of responsible delegates speaking in the name of their respective Governments is maintained. For that principle to be as effective as it should be it is clearly necessary that the head of the delegation at any rate should be a Cabinet Minister fully cognizant of the mind of his Ministerial colleagues. The ideal representation was most nearly attained at the Fifth Assembly in 1924, when some seven Prime Ministers and sixteen Foreign Ministers attended the whole or some part of the Assembly discussions. It may be added that under the Covenant women are qualified equally with men to hold any position in the League, including that of delegate at the Assembly. No nation, however, sent a woman delegate to any of the first five Assemblies, though the three Scandinavian countries, Great Britain, Australia and Rumania regularly included a woman among their delegates-substitute.

As has been mentioned already, the Assembly meets regularly at Geneva every September, the sittings beginning on the first Monday in the month. Its first business is to verify the credentials of all the delegates, i.e. to make sure that they have been appointed in proper form by their Governments, and elect a President for the month's sessions. There is a different President each year, and it is usually found convenient to choose a representative of a State not represented on the Council, since the Council is constantly in session during the Assembly month, and a delegate could not be at the same time at the Presidential desk in the Assembly and at his place at the Council table. The first five Presidents were M. Paul Hymans (Belgium), Jonkheer van Karnebeeck (Holland), Señor Agustin Edwards (Chile), Señor Torriente (Cuba) and M. Guiseppe Motta (Switzerland). The first week or so of the discussions is devoted mainly to considering a report by the Secretary-General on the work of the Council, which means in effect the whole work of the League, in the twelve months just concluded, and at the same time the business of the Assembly is shared out among six large committees, on each of which every delegation is entitled to a place, whose business is to thrash out each subject in detail and report finally to the full Assembly, which can usually accept the conclusions as they stand, thereby saving itself a great deal of time and trouble. The six classes of questions dealt with by the six committees are (with slight variations from year to year) :

I. Legal and Constitutional questions.
II. The League's Technical Organizations (e.g. the Economic Health and Transit Commissions).
III. Disarmament.
IV. The League's Budget.
V. Humanitarian questions.
VI. Political questions (including mandates).

Questions can be placed on the agenda at the request of a Government, or by decision of the Assembly itself, or as a legacy from the preceding Assembly.

Though the Assembly may be likened roughly to a Parliament, and the Council to a Cabinet, the analogy can easily be misleading and must not be pressed. Some questions (e.g. the admission of new members) are assigned by the Covenant definitely to the Assembly and some (e.g. mandates) definitely to the Council, while some (e.g. amendments of the Covenant) call for action by both bodies. As a matter of practice the Council tends to become very much the executive of the Assembly, for the simple reason that it is small enough to meet often and be called together in case of need at short notice, while so large a body as the Assembly is never likely to sit, except in some cases of special emergency, oftener than once a year. (The original framers of the Covenant thought it quite likely that it would only meet about once in four years.) The great value of the Assembly is as a forum of free and public discussion—in its first five sessions it has never held a private sitting—and most of its decisions take the form of a recommendation to the Council to get some desired action taken.

The Council itself is limited in numbers, partly in the interest of convenience and efficiency and partly to give the more important States a predominance which they do not enjoy in the Assembly, where every State sends three delegates and every delegation has one vote. In the Council Great Britain, France, Italy and Japan have permanent seats, and a certain number of other members are elected annually by the Assembly. The expedient of putting all States on the same level in the Assembly, but giving the greater ones the advantage of permanent places in the Council, is a little like that adopted by the framers of the Constitution of the United States, who gave each State, great or small, two seats in the Senate, but provided that representation in the House should be on the basis of population.

Under the Covenant the " non-permanent " members of the Council, i.e. those elected annually by the Assembly, were to be four in number, and the first four—Belgium, Spain, Brazil and Greece—were actually named in the Covenant itself. At the First Assembly in 1920, China was substituted for Greece. At the Second Assembly all the four non-permanent members then sitting were re-elected. At the Third their number was increased from four to six, Belgium, Spain, Brazil and China being re-elected and Sweden and Uruguay added. At the Fourth Czechoslovakia was substituted for China, and at the Fifth the six then sitting were re-elected. It was never intended that the permanent members of the Council should all be Allied Powers. The hope, on the contrary, was and is that the United States, Germany and Russia will all have permanent seats on the Council as soon as they become members of the League.

The Council meets at least four times a year, in March, June, September and December, and as much oftener as the business arising may require, the different members presiding in turn at successive meetings. The sittings are usually held at Geneva, but about once a year the Council meets in some national capital, such as London, Paris, Rome or Brussels, largely with the idea of enabling the countries concerned to become acquainted with its work at first hand. Most of the business is conducted in public, with the Press of the world present, though the Council has always the right to sit in private, which it regularly does when dealing with certain kinds of business. It is clearly impossible, for example, when some important appointment is being made, to discuss the personal merits and demerits of the different candidates in public.

While the actual membership of the Council is at present ten—four permanent members and six non-permanent—there is frequently a larger number of representatives than that at the table, for under Article IV of the Covenant any League State is entitled to sit during a discussion of any question specially affecting it. Thus when the reconstruction of Austria was under consideration, there appeared at the Council table representatives not only of Austria itself, but of the neighbouring Little Entente States, Czechoslovakia (which was not at that time a member of the Council), Jugoslavia and Rumania. In the same way, when the affairs of Danzig are under consideration there are called to the table the High Commissioner of Danzig (who is a League official) and representatives of the Free City and of Poland. Non-members like Turkey have also sat temporarily on the Council during the discussion of differences that have arisen between them and a State member of the League.

At both Assembly and Council every State has one vote, and decisions, except on secondary points like questions of procedure, must be unanimous. Such a stipulation may seem a fatal bar to effective agreement. On that there are two comments to be made. In the first place the provision is inevitable. Without it there would have been no League at all, for no State would have been ready to join if there were any possibility of its being coerced by a majority vote of its fellow-members into doing something it preferred not to do. That is true of every international con-ference. At the Washington Arms Conference in 1921–2, for example, President Harding pointed out that what had been achieved had been, and could only have been, achieved by the free agreement of every State concerned. It is the same in the Assembly and the Council of the League. Problems are thrashed out till general agreement can be reached. Conces-sions are made by one State, the moral pressure of public opinion is brought to bear on another, and in the end when, after agreement has been definitely established, a vote is taken, it serves as little more than a convenient means of registering the conclusions reached in the discussion. In the Council every decision except on questions of procedure has to be unanimous. In the Assembly the principal exception to the unanimity rule is the provision whereby a two-thirds majority is sufficient to elect new members of the League.

The language difficulty is, of course, bound to be perpetual at Geneva. Fortunately, there are two languages, English and French, which hold an admitted predominance in the world, and they have been adopted as the two official languages of the League. That means that every speech is delivered in one of those tongues and translated into the other by a member of the League's remarkably competent corps of interpreters. Similarly every document issued by the League appears both in English and French. Taking the Assembly as a whole, French is much more often heard than English, the principal English speeches coming from representatives of the British Dominions, the Scandinavian countries, China and Japan. There is a provision that any delegate may speak in his own tongue if he himself provides an interpreter who will translate into either English or French. Occasional advantage has been taken of this by Spanish, Austrian (German-speaking), Irish and Abyssinian delegates.

The Council, while it consists always of representatives of the four permanent members and the six non-permanent, does not always consist of the same personalities, for though each Member-State naturally tries to send the same representative every time, that is not always possible. Changes of Government in a country commonly mean a change in League representation, and even the same Government often changes its delegate. Great Britain, for example, has been variously represented—under the Coalition Government by Lord Balfour, Mr. Fisher and Mr. Harmsworth, and under the different Conservative Governments of Mr. Bonar Law and Mr. Baldwin by Lord Cecil, Mr. Edward Wood and Mr. Austen Chamberlain. Council representatives, moreover, though they are all experienced diplomatists, are not technical experts, and when technical questions have to be handled, as they constantly have, expert advice is usually needed. That is supplied by what are known as the League's " Technical Organizations," a series of very competent committees, including among their members some of the first authorities in the world on the subjects with which they deal. Two of these committees, the Permanent Advisory Commission of Armaments and the Mandates Commission, are definitely provided for in Articles IX and XXII of the Covenant, and a number of others—those, for example, on financial and economic questions, on transit questions, public health, the dangerous drug traffic, the traffic in women and children—have been created to assist the League in discharging the duties devolving on it in these various fields under Article XXIII. Yet another committee, that on intellectual co-operation, is the outcome of a decision of the Second Assembly, that the League should venture spontaneously into this new sphere of activity. In point of fact some of the most important work the League has ever done has been carried through almost entirely by one or other of the technical committees. That is most notably the case with the reconstruction schemes in Austria,

Hungary and Greece, all the details of which were worked out by the Financial Commission, though all final decisions were taken by and with the authority of the Council.

The machinery of the League (disregarding for the moment the International Labour Organization and the Permanent Court of International Justice) consists, then, of an Assembly comprising three delegates from each State member of the League, a Council comprising one representative from each of ten States, a number of technical commissions to advise the Council, and a permanent Secretariat, on whose ceaseless if unobtrusive activities Assembly, Council and commissions all depend for the success of their own endeavours.

The Secretariat is the distinctive feature of the League. Nothing like it has ever existed before in the international sphere. The precedent for its creation may be said to have been set to some extent by the temporary secretariat created in connection with the Supreme War Council of the Allies in the later stages of the war. But the precedent was not followed closely. The War Council secretariat consisted of officials from a number of different nations lent by them and working together temporarily at Versailles. It was suggested at first that the League Secretariat should be constituted on much the same lines. Other, and unquestionably wiser, counsels, however, prevailed, and the Secretariat as it exists to-day is something much more than a collection of national units. It is itself a remarkable and unique international unit. Its members, from the Secretary-General downwards, are the servants of the League of Nations and of no one else. They are drawn from practically every nation, included in the League, and from at least one, the

United States, still outside it. When you enter the hall of the large hotel on the shore of Lake Geneva where the Secretariat is housed, the first man (or for that matter woman) you meet is likely to be an Italian, the second a Japanese, the third a Canadian, the fourth a Spaniard, the fifth a Czechoslovakian, and so forth. All of them retain their own nationality, but none of them owns any official allegiance to the Government of his country. Their allegiance is to the League alone. They are appointed by the League and paid by the League, and their first and last duty is to do the League's work. In their day-to-day activity they work side by side as servants of the League, with differences of nationality almost wholly forgotten. Rarely will two Englishmen, or two Frenchmen, or two members of any other nationality be found working together (except that an official usually prefers, as a matter of convenience, to have a secretary of his own nationality). The head of one particular section, for example, is a Frenchman, who has as the principal members of his staff a Greek, an Italian, an Englishman, a Swiss and a Czechoslovakian. In all other sections the same mixture of nationalities exists. The result is a constant and invaluable interchange of points of view and the steady development of something like a real international outlook.

The work of the Secretariat in relation to the League may be compared broadly to the work of the Government Departments in Whitehall in relation to the British Parliament and Cabinet. Every decision of the League, and every duty laid on it by the Covenant, involves a large amount of correspondence and administrative work, and for that the Secretariat is responsible. It is, of course, divided up into departments, of which the principal are (at the end of 1924):

the Political, with a Frenchman as its head ; the Technical Organizations, under an Englishman ; Minorities, under a Norwegian ; Mandates, under an Italian ; Health, under a Pole ; Social Questions, under an Englishwoman ; Information (i.e. Press publicity), under a Frenchman ; Legal, under a Dutchman ; Armaments, under a Spaniard. The first Secretary-General (the chief official of the League), Sir Eric Drummond, who was formerly a member of the British Foreign Office staff, was appointed by an Annexe of the Covenant itself. He is responsible for appointing members of the Secretariat, subject to the approval of the Council.

All this, of course, means money. There are the Secretariat salaries to be paid. There is a large sum for travelling expenses, not merely for Secretariat members visiting other countries on League business, but for members of League Commissions who have to come to Geneva or some other centre to sit. There is the rent of buildings, or its equivalent, the interest on loans raised to buy buildings. There is a formidable item for cabling and postage and printing ; and there are, of course, numberless lesser expenses. Altogether it is astonishing that the League manages to spend as little as it does, the total of its budget expenditure for 1925, including the whole cost of the International Labour Organization and the Permanent Court of International Justice, being 22,658,138 " gold francs," or just under £900,000.

That sum has to be raised by contributions from the fifty-five States at present (1924-5) members of the League. But clearly the expense could not be shared equally. To expect the same subscription from Albania and Great Britain would be manifestly unreasonable. At the same time it is no easy matter to decide how far and in what proportion contributions should vary. When the League was formed some temporary basis had to be provided till a proper scale could be framed, and it was accordingly decided to work for the moment on the only international scale then existing, that of subscriptions to the Universal Postal Union, under which States were assessed in four or five different categories according to their assumed capacity to pay.

The Universal Postal Union scale, however, was soon found to be unsatisfactory, and a strong committee was appointed by the Assembly to draft an alternative. The principle adopted by it consists in rating each member State at a certain number of units, ranging, as things stand, from 88 in the case of Great Britain down to 1 in the case of Albania, San Domingo and one or two other penniless States. As examples of intermediate ratings it may be mentioned that France pays 78 units, Italy 61, China 50, Spain 40, Brazil and Czechoslovakia 33, Poland 25, South Africa 15, Norway 10, Persia 5, Abyssinia 2, and Panama 1. The value of a unit represents, of course, the total expenditure divided by the total number of units (both of which may vary from year to year). For 1925 the total expenditure was, as already stated, just under £900,000, and the total number of units 935. Each unit, therefore, has the value of a little less than £1,000, and Great Britain's contribution of 88 units works out at an expenditure in sterling of rather under £86,000. It may be mentioned, for purposes of comparison, that the cost to the Exchequer of the Natural History Museum in South Kensington in 1924–5 was £98,807, and of the Victoria and Albert Museum £141,038.

CHAPTER IV

THE LEAGUE AND LABOUR

The International Labour Organization—How it was created—Its Constitution—Its Functions—Its Methods—Its Achievements.

THE League of Nations Budget, as has been shown already, covers not only the manifold activities of the League proper (as it is commonly conceived), but also the International Labour Organization and the Per-. manent Court of International Justice. Strictly speaking, both Labour Organization and Court are integral parts of the League, but they are both autonomous, the Labour Organization being subject to no sort of control, except in the matter of finance, by the Assembly or Council of the League, and the Court, as might be expected of a judicial body, being similarly independent.

The Permanent Court, as will be seen in the following chapter, was created by the League. The Labour Organization was not. It is separate from the League not only in operation but in origin. The only reference to it in the Covenant is contained in that clause in Article XXIII whereby League members agree that they will

" endeavour to secure and maintain fair and humane conditions of labour for men, women and children, both in their own countries and in all countries to which their commercial and industrial relations extend, and for that purpose will establish and maintain the necessary international organizations."

34

As a matter of fact the necessary organizations were already established, on paper at any rate, when the League came into existence ; or, rather, the birth of the two institutions, the political and the industrial, was simultaneous, for while Articles 1-26 of the Treaty of Versailles brought the League of Nations into being, another and longer section of the Treaty, consisting of Articles 387-426, provided for the creation of a permanent Labour Organization to which all original and future members of the League should belong.

All members of the League are therefore members of the I.L.O. So are certain other States. Thus Germany was admitted at the first International Labour Conference held in Washington in 1919 (before the League was established in concrete form). From that time she has taken an active and prominent part in the work of the Organization.

The constitution of the I.L.O. roughly corresponds to that of the League, as the following comparison will show :

League.	I.L.O.
Assembly	General Conference
Council	Governing Body
Secretariat	International Labour Office

Before details of the I.L.O.'s constitution are considered its essential difference from the League must be realized. The League, it has been seen, consists entirely of the representatives of Governments. The Labour Organization strikes a new note in international associations by bringing together on an equal footing representatives of Governments, representatives of employers and representatives of labour. In the General Conference (corresponding to the League Assembly) there sit four delegates from each State,

two of them respresenting the respective Governments
and one each the employers and the workers, the two
latter being appointed by the Governments in agreement with the principal employers' and workers'
organizations in their country. The Governing Body
(corresponding to the League Council) consists of
twenty-four persons, of whom twelve represent Governments, six employers and six labour. The latter are
elected by the employers and labour delegates to the
General Conference. The former consist of nominees
of the eight principal industrial States (it is for the
League Council to decide, in case of need, which these
are) and another four chosen by the full body of
Government delegates (other than those of the eight
States mentioned above) to the General Conference.
It will be seen that an analogy is thus established
with the permanent and non-permanent members of
the League Council. The International Labour Office
corresponds to the League Secretariat and fulfils much
the same functions. Its head is termed Director, the
first holder of that office being M. Albert Thomas,
Minister of Munitions in France for some time during
the war. The Labour Office is now by far the best-
stocked repository of industrial information in the
world, and its monthly *International Labour Review*
and weekly *Industrial and Labour Information* are
proportionately valuable. It also publishes from time
to time comprehensive reports on many aspects of
industry, compiled from an international standpoint.
  The Organization's main work, for which the
collection and collation of world information is an
essential preliminary, consists in the framing and
the adoption at its annual conferences of " Conventions " on industrial questions or of " Recommendations " as to the nature and aim of domestic

legislation in the different countries. Of these the Conventions are the more important. They are not in themselves binding on Governments, and clearly could not be, since they can be adopted by a two-thirds majority of a body only half of whose members are Government delegates, but every Government is pledged (by Article 405 of the Treaty of Versailles) to bring a Draft Convention within twelve months, or in exceptional cases eighteen months, " before the authority or authorities within whose competence the matter lies, for the enactment of legislation or other action." It is clearly intended that Conventions shall be ratified, and the legislation of the different countries brought into conformity with them, but all a Government is actually pledged to do is to *submit* all Conventions to its legislative authority. It is not under even a moral obligation to work for their adoption, except in so far as its delegates may have voted for them at the Conference where they were approved, but once they are adopted it is under a quite specific obligation to enforce them. The Convention, when ratified, becomes, in effect, a Treaty.

A Recommendation, equally with a Draft Convention, has to be laid before the competent authority within eighteen months. But it has not to be ratified ; the State has only to inform the Secretary-General of the League of the action taken. Thus whilst a Convention when ratified imposes a binding obligation, a Recommendation is to be taken rather as a guide in the passing of national legislation.

Down to the end of 1924 six General Conferences had been held, and seventeen Conventions approved. The main agreements reached were :

WASHINGTON, 1919 : *Conventions* on 8-hour day and 48-hour week ; provision against unemployment ; employment of women before and after child-birth; employment of women at night; minimum age of children in industry; night work of young persons. *Recommendations* on public employment exchanges; reciprocity of treatment of foreign workers; prevention of anthrax; protection of women and children against lead-poisoning; establishment of Government Health Services; and application of Berne (1906) Convention prohibiting the use of white phosphorus in the manufacture of matches.

GENOA, 1920: *Conventions* on age of employment of children at sea; unemployment indemnity in case of shipwreck; facilities for finding employment for seamen. *Recommendations* on limitation of hours of work in the fishing industry; their limitation in inland navigation; national seamen's codes; unemployment insurance for seamen.

GENEVA, 1921: *Conventions* on right of association of agricultural workers; workmen's compensation in agriculture; minimum age of children in agriculture; white lead in painting; minimum age of employment as trimmers and stokers at sea; medical examination of young persons at sea; and weekly rest in industry. *Recommendations* on technical agricultural education; prevention of unemployment in agriculture; social insurance in agriculture; night work of young persons and of women in agriculture, and protection of women before and after child-birth; living-in conditions of agricultural workers; and the weekly rest in commercial establishments.

GENEVA, 1922: *One Recommendation* on statistical and other information about emigration.

GENEVA, 1923: *One Recommendation* on the general principles for the organization of systems of inspection to secure the enforcement of laws and regulations for the protection of the workers.

GENEVA, 1924: *Two Conventions* provisionally adopted on the weekly suspension of work in certain glass-making processes and the prohibition of night work in bakeries. These, together with a Convention and a Recommendation, also provisionally adopted, dealing with equality of treatment of foreign workers as regards workmen's compensation, will be finally decided at the 1925 Conference. One Recommendation was, however, adopted finally, with regard to the utilization of workers' spare time.

The ratification of Conventions is never a very rapid process, even when they are non-contentious, and some of the I.L.O. Conventions have caused subsequent misgivings even to Governments whose delegates have voted for them. So it came about that at the end of 1924 the British Government, whilst it had ratified in all eight Conventions, had ratified neither of the two 1919 Conventions on hours and on rest at child-birth (the " Maternity Convention," as it is commonly called), nor the White Lead Paint Convention. The record of other countries is in some cases better, in others worse, and not the least of the duties of the Labour Office is to keep constantly before Governments their duty in the matter of ratification. That real progress has been made is, however, shown by the fact that in October 1921 the total of ratifications formally registered was 30 ; at the end of 1922 it was 63 ; at the end of 1923 it was 92 ; whilst at the end of 1924 it was 142.

It is not to be expected that the Labour Organization should in its early stages do a great deal to change the industrial conditions in countries where, as in Great Britain, high standards have already been achieved. What is hoped is that through the working of the I.L.O. conditions in backward countries, particularly in the Far East, may be gradually levelled up. That, in point of fact, is actually happening. Japan, India, China and Persia have all proved responsive not merely to the influence of the annual I.L.O. Conferences but to the friendly and semi-official representations of the Labour Office. In India hours of labour have been materially shortened and the minimum age for the employment of children raised (from nine years to twelve). In Japan, similarly, the employment of children under twelve has been prohibited. In China hours and age decrees have been promulgated, but in the present political state of the country the enforcement of any such measures is difficult. In Persia the conditions of child labour have been greatly improved.

Like the League, the Labour Organization has equipped itself with a number of expert committees to study particular questions, notably the Joint Maritime Commission (on labour conditions at sea), the Commission on Unemployment, the International Emigration Commission, the Advisory Committees on Agriculture, on Anthrax and on Industrial Hygiene. In addition, the Organization co-operates actively with a number of League Committees. It has, for example, a representative on the Mandates Commission and the Committee on Intellectual Co-operation. While the Temporary Mixed Armaments Commission was in existence the Labour Organization supplied six of its members. It also took over bodily from the League in 1924 responsibility for the refugee work carried on till that time for the League by Dr. Nansen.

Again, like the League, the International Labour Organization cannot be successful in its efforts to "level up" conditions of labour unless it has the support of an informed public opinion in the advanced and also, in some degree at least, in the backward countries. But even as things are the general discussions at the Labour Conferences, carried on by the persons actually responsible for framing and administering industrial regulations in different countries, are of great and increasing value and may often be as important in their ultimate effects as the adoption of formal Conventions.

CHAPTER V

THE COURT OF INTERNATIONAL JUSTICE

Its origin—Appointment of Judges—Compulsory Jurisdiction
—Advisory Opinions—Great Powers before the Court.

THE third of the main organisms of which the League
of Nations consists is the Permanent Court of International Justice, established since 1922 in the building
known as the Peace Palace at The Hague. The Court,
unlike the League and the Labour Organization, was
not a direct creation of the Covenant or of the Treaty
of Versailles. Article XIV of the Covenant provided
that plans for the establishment of such a Court
should be formulated and submitted by the League
Council to League members. The work was put in
hand in time for the full statutes of the Court to be
approved by the Assembly of 1920, and the first
judges were elected during the Assembly of 1921,
with the result that the Court itself came formally
into existence in January 1922.

The Permanent Court, therefore, was created
directly by the League, and it is doubtful whether it
could have been created in any other way. More
than one previous attempt had been made, but all
had broken down through failure to agree on the
method of the appointment of judges. The Great
Powers always insisted on a predominant voice in the
election, a claim which the smaller States would never
consent to recognize. The establishment of the League,

with its extensive provisions for the settlement of disputes without war, first of all re-emphasized the need for an International Court of Justice, secondly did much to create an atmosphere in which agreement on such a matter as the appointment of judges was likely to be reached, and thirdly provided a practical and generally-accepted method for carrying the election through. That method consisted in separate and simultaneous elections by the League Council, in which at that time the Great Powers held four out of eight places, and by the Assembly, in which all States were on an equality. Only those candidates chosen by both bodies were to be declared elected, and the voting was to continue till Council and Assembly were agreed on all the judges. The arrangement worked with unexpected smoothness. Eleven judges had to be appointed and nine names were found to figure on the first lists both of Council and Assembly, whose members were voting simultaneously in different buildings in Geneva. Agreement on the two remaining judges and the four deputy-judges was quickly reached and the machinery of the Court was complete when the 1921 Assembly rose.

The Court, as has been said, is established at The Hague, a course dictated by consideration partly for the great traditions of Dutch jurisprudence and partly for the American donors of the Peace Palace. In the opinion of many it would have been better to mass all the League institutions at Geneva, and the choice of The Hague has created in some minds a confusion between the Court and the old Hague arbitration panels, with which it has in reality no connection at all. It consists of eleven judges and four deputy-judges, who are paid adequate salaries out of League funds. They have regular sessions and can

be convened at other times if urgent business arises.
Decisions are given, as in practically all Courts of
Appeal, by a majority vote.

Only Governments can appear as parties before the
Court. If an individual has an international grievance
he must persuade his Government to espouse his
cause. (This happened in 1924 in the case of a Greek
subject who desired to make claims against the British
Government as mandatory of Palestine. The Greek
Government appeared before the Court on his behalf.)
With certain exceptions, moreover, only those cases
go to the Court which *both* parties to the dispute
agree to submit to it. One party, that is to say,
cannot require its opponent to go before the Court at
all. The exceptions to this rule are, however, important and may soon be much more important. In
the first place, it is now becoming increasingly the
practice to insert in international treaties a clause
providing that any dispute under the treaty shall be
settled by the Permanent Court. In such a case the
parties to the treaty are bound, in case of dispute,
to go before the Court. In the second place a number
of States, taking advantage of an " optional clause "
inserted in the statutes of the Court, have agreed
among themselves that they will *always* refer to the
Court any dispute arising between them if it is of a
character suitable for decision by the Court. By the
end of 1924 fifteen States had signed and ratified
the optional clause. None of the Great Powers had
down to that date accepted this universal reference
of all suitable disputes to the Court, but an essential
part of the Geneva Protocol, approved in principle
by the 1924 Assembly, was the acceptance of the
optional clause by all States ratifying the Protocol.
France in that connection did actually sign the

optional clause, but at the end of 1924 had not ratified it.

Reference to disputes suitable for decision by the Court needs a word of explanation. The Court exists to interpret and administer law. It deals therefore only with questions which arise out of an alleged breach of international law or of a definite treaty obligation, and one or two other classes of dispute known technically as "justiciable." Many of the questions referred to the League for settlement, e.g. the Upper Silesia division, or the Iraq boundary, or the Memel port question, the Court would be quite incompetent to handle.

As to the Court and its actual work, a word on the composition of the bench is necessary. The eleven judges and four deputy-judges hold office for nine years, vacancies occurring through death or retirement being filled (by the Council and Assembly) as they arise. The bench consisted, in 1924, of the following jurists :

> Señor Altamira (Spain).
> Signor Anzilotti (Italy).
> Señor Epitacio de Pessoa (Brazil).
> Señor de Bustamante (Cuba).
> Lord Finlay (Great Britain).
> Dr. Loder (Netherlands).
> Dr. Bassett Moore (United States).
> M. Oda (Japan).
> M. Weiss (France)
> M. Nyholm (Denmark)
> M. Huber (Switzerland).

with the following deputy judges :

> M. Negulesco (Rumania).
> M. Wang Chung-hui (China).
> M. Yovanovitch (Jugoslavia).
> M. Beichmann (Norway).

It will be observed that an American jurist was appointed, though the United States is a member neither of the League nor of the Court. As President of the Court Dr. Loder, of Holland, was elected for the first three years and Dr. Max Huber, of Switzerland, for the second three.

The main business of the Court has been twofold, the settlement of actual disputes referred to it direct, and the formulation of advisory opinions on questions submitted to it by the League Council. The latter have been the more numerous and may play quite as large a part in the settlement of a dispute. Down to the end of 1924, the Court had given nine advisory opinions and three judgments. Among the former the most important was a decision, which ended a protracted controversy between Great Britain and France, on the question whether the conscription by France of British subjects in French protectorates (Morocco and Tunis) could be regarded as falling within the domestic jurisdiction of France. The British Attorney-General appeared at The Hague to support the British contention which was upheld by the Court. France thereupon came to terms on the main issue.

In the case of the ss. *Wimbledon* in 1923 (the issue being whether in spite of the Kiel Canal having been declared by the Treaty of Versailles open to the ships of all nations, Germany was justified on grounds of neutrality in refusing passage to a vessel laden with arms for Poland, which was then at war with Russia), a German judge took his seat on the bench, in accordance with the regulation by which every party to a dispute before the Court is entitled to have one of its own nationals on the bench. The case was brought by the Allied Powers, and the verdict went against Germany by nine votes to three.

Great Britain, as the Power administering the Palestine mandate, was a party to a case arising out of the claims of a Greek national in respect of pre-war concessions in Palestine. Two cases in which the Court gave advisory opinions in favour of Germany against Poland have also some significance.

Though the Permanent Court has not so far had to handle any question of the first magnitude, its position as the ultimate tribunal of appeal in all international controversies that can be decided on legal grounds is firmly established, and the Court is held in as much respect in America as in Europe. It may be mentioned that the statutes were so drawn that membership is open not merely to all States members of the League but to any non-members appearing in the first Annexe to the Covenant (i.e. those States which intended in 1919 to become members of the League). This includes the United States, which can therefore associate itself officially with the Court at any moment without joining the League. As the codification of international law foreshadowed by a resolution of the Fifth Assembly progresses, the scope of the Court's jurisdiction will be substantially extended.

CHAPTER VI

HOW DISPUTES ARE SETTLED

Three methods—Court, Arbitration or Council Inquiry—
Domestic Jurisdiction—The Covenant and the Protocol—
The Vilna Question—The Aaland Islands Dispute—Upper
Silesia—Jugoslavia and Albania—Memel—Corfu—Iraq.

ONE of the main purposes of the League of Nations
is the settlement of international disputes by other
means than war. A considerable proportion of the
Covenant is devoted to the establishment of machinery
to that end; the agreements freely entered into in
this respect by the States signing the Covenant mark
a substantial advance in international practice; and
the application of the agreements has, in a number
of cases arising during the League's first five years of
existence, been sufficiently effective to prove that the
standard set in the Covenant was not too high for
practical observance.

It is necessary to be quite clear about what the
Covenant does and does not prescribe in the matter of
disputes, particularly since the Geneva Protocol of
1924 cannot be understood without a detailed comparison of its provisions with those of the Covenant.
The Covenant does not profess to impose compulsory
arbitration in any full sense. Its essential principles—
though it goes a good deal beyond them in certain
directions—are conference and delay. Every State,
that is to say, binds itself not to go to war till it has

submitted its dispute to some form of inquiry, and undertakes even after that to wait at least three months before striking a blow. These provisions combine the main principles of a number of pre-war arbitration agreements between different nations dealing specifically with questions of a legal or " justiciable " character, and of the so-called Bryan treaties, concluded between the United States and some thirty other Powers, providing that every dispute of any kind shall be made the subject of inquiry, the parties to the dispute undertaking to refrain from war for at least twelve months while the inquiry is in progress.

The Covenant provides three methods of settlement. Its provisions are briefly as follows :

(1) Disputes suitable for the Permanent Court of International Justice to go to the Court.

(2) Other disputes to be made the subject of arbitration by agreement between the parties.

(3) Failing either of these courses, the whole matter to be brought before the League Council.

Every State member of the League has pledged itself (by Article XII [1] of the Covenant) to follow one of these courses, and they have, farther than that, gone some way towards pledging themselves to accept the verdict given. The position in that regard is that in the case of disputes decided by either (1) the Permanent Court, or (2) Arbitration, " the members of the League agree that they will carry out in full good faith any award that may be rendered, and that they

[1] " The Members of the League agree that if there should arise between them any dispute likely to lead to a rupture, they will submit the matter either to arbitration or judicial settlement or to inquiry by the Council, and they agree in no case to resort to war until three months after the award by the arbitrators or the judicial decision or the report by the Council.":

will not resort to war against a member of the League which complies therewith " (Article XIII). The latter provision means that the loser of a case may not make armed resistance to a State that has gained the verdict and is taking steps to secure the benefit of it. It is added, moreover, a little vaguely that " in the event of any failure to carry out such an award the Council shall propose what steps should be taken to give effect thereto."

Inquiry by the Council stands on a different footing from adjudication by the Court or by arbitrators. In the former case the obligation to accept a verdict exists only when the case is so clear that the whole ten members of the Council are unanimous about it. If they are divided the only obligation imposed is to wait three months before going to war. Even in the case of a unanimous verdict there is no explicit undertaking on the part of the loser to carry it out. What is stipulated is that no member of the League (including, of course, the loser) shall go to war with a party which complies with the Council's recommendations. Parties to a dispute are entitled to sit on the Council while their dispute is being considered, but their votes are not reckoned, whether they are regular members of the Council or not. Non-members of the League can be treated (Article XVII) for purposes of a dispute as though they were members. Article XVI provides that a State which goes to war in violation of its pledges under the arbitration clauses of the Covenant shall be regarded as a common enemy of the whole League and subjected, as circumstances may demand, to (1) boycott, (2) blockade, (3) if necessary, military pressure.

It is to be observed that all disputes under this section of the Covenant must be " international," i.e.

4

not arise out of action (such as the imposition of tariffs or the exclusion of would-be immigrants), which every nation is recognized as fully entitled to take without interference from any outside Power. In such cases—involving questions of "domestic jurisdiction" as they are called—neither the Court nor arbitrators nor the Council can impose any settlement, unless indeed both parties voluntarily agree to such a course in advance. But not only questions of domestic jurisdiction, but any question whatever which "threatens to disturb international peace or the good understanding between nations on which peace depends" can be brought before the Council, not merely by one of the States immediately concerned, but by any member of the League, under the invaluable Article XI.[1]   In such a case the Council's function consists in thrashing out the whole matter with the disputants and relying on its moral influence to induce them to accept the settlement it suggests. Domestic jurisdiction questions, like any others, can be raised under Article XI, and it rests with the Council itself to decide whether a question is "domestic" or not. On such a matter, however, it would usually take the advice of the Court.

It is perhaps relevant to point out here where the Geneva Protocol of 1924 went beyond the Covenant.

---

[1] "Any war or threat of war, whether immediately affecting any of the Members of the League or not, is hereby declared a matter of concern to the whole League, and the League shall take any action that may be deemed wise and effectual to safeguard the peace of nations. In case any such emergency should arise, the Secretary-General shall on the request of any Member of the League forthwith summon a meeting of the Council.

⊢ "It is also declared to be the friendly right of each Member of the League to bring to the attention of the Assembly or of the Council any circumstance whatever affecting international relations which threatens to disturb international peace or the good understanding between nations upon which peace depends."

Its aim was to secure that *all* disputes between nations should be settled without war, and it therefore set itself to close the door left open in the case in which the Council fails to reach unanimity. Here the Protocol provides, briefly, that as a last resort the Council shall itself appoint a board of impartial arbitrators to whom the dispute shall be referred and whose verdict shall be final and binding. Other provisions of the Geneva Protocol are more fully dealt with in the following chapter.

After this necessary explanation of the League's methods of settlement a few examples of disputes actually handled by the League will be worth examining. The cases chosen have been selected less for their intrinsic importance than for the illustration they furnish of the variety and flexibility of the League's methods of dealing with such questions. The Council, when a dispute comes before it, follows no rule-of-thumb procedure, but holds itself entirely free to take such steps as the circumstances of the particular question before it suggest. That is shown clearly by the following examples :

(1) *The Vilna Question.*—A dispute between Poland and Lithuania, brought before the League by Poland in September 1920. Sporadic warfare between the two countries was in progress, due largely to the fact that the frontier between them had never been definitely delimited by the Allied Powers, in whose hands the matter lay. The League Council sent a commission to the frontier, and an armistice was arranged, but immediately afterwards the town of Vilna, then held by Lithuania, was seized by the Polish General Zeligowski, whose act was disavowed by the Polish

Government, which, however, took no steps against him. The question of the ownership of Vilna now became the main issue, and it is to be noted that though Poland had put itself clearly in the wrong, that did not necessarily give Lithuania a right to the town. The League's intervention put an end to the fighting, which was never renewed, and after long and patient negotiations a full plan of settlement was drawn up by M. Paul Hymans, acting as mediator on behalf of the Council. This was unanimously approved by the Council, and therefore under Article XV of the Covenant if one of the two parties had accepted it, the other would have been compelled to acquiesce. Neither of them, however, saw fit to do so, and the Council had finally to abandon its efforts. It thus did not effect a settlement, but the application to the dispute of the method of conference allowed hot blood to cool, and fighting between Poland and Lithuania was never renewed.

(2) *The Aaland Islands Question.*—The Aaland Islands lie in the Baltic Sea, midway between Sweden and Finland. They are strategically important because they are capable of commanding both the Swedish capital, Stockholm, on the one hand, and the entrance of the Gulf of Finland on the other. When Finland gained its independence from Russia in 1918, the Aaland Islands, which had for over a century formed part of Finland (and therefore of Russia), but whose population was for the most part Swedish in origin, demanded to be transferred to Swedish sovereignty. Finland rejected and Sweden supported their request, with the result that a serious

dispute arose between the two countries. This was brought before the League in June 1920 by the British Government, acting under Article XI of the Covenant. Finland at once claimed that the matter was one within her domestic jurisdiction, and that, therefore, the Council was not competent to act. The Permanent Court of International Justice not being then in existence, the Council appointed a special commission of jurists (one French, one Dutch and one Swiss) to investigate Finland's contention. They reported against it and the Council therefore continued its work, appointing a new commission (one American, one Belgian and one Swiss) to examine the whole question and recommend a solution. The commission visited Sweden, Finland and the Aaland Islands themselves, and submitted recommendations providing that the islands should remain under Finnish sovereignty, but should enjoy a large measure of autonomy and be permanently demilitarized. These proposals were unanimously approved by the Council, whose findings were loyally accepted by both Sweden and Finland. A complete settlement was therefore effected.

(3) *Upper Silesia Question.*—Under Article 88 of the Treaty of Versailles the territory known as Upper Silesia was to be divided between Germany and Poland in accordance with a vote of the inhabitants. The vote, or plebiscite, was taken in May 1921, but the Allied Powers, with whom the decision rested, were unable to agree as to what line of division the plebiscite results indicated. They therefore referred the whole question to the League, undertaking to accept whatever solution the League

Council might advise. It is to be noted that the Council was not invited, and was not at liberty, to propose an ideal solution of the Upper Silesian question. Its task consisted simply of deciding where, in the light of the plebiscite results, the line of division between Poland and Germany in Upper Silesia should run. No line could be satisfactory, for the population was so mixed that any line was bound to leave large numbers of Germans under Polish sovereignty and large numbers of Poles under German. The Council, after taking expert advice, drew the best line it could, and the Allied Powers immediately accepted it. The important feature of the Council's action, however, was that it did not leave the matter there. Having been compelled by the Treaty of Versailles to see a political frontier drawn through Upper Silesia, the League determined to do everything possible to prevent the frontier from shattering the economic life of the region, as so many frontiers had done elsewhere. Accordingly, instead of stopping when it had done its appointed work of delimiting the political boundary, the Council proceeded to recommend that arrangements should be made whereby the railway system of Upper Silesia should continue to be worked as a unit, German currency remain legal tender through the whole area, the water and electricity supplies be maintained on the existing basis, social legislation and industrial insurance arrangements be preserved on both sides of the frontier, and the free passage of both Poles and Germans in either direction be facilitated in every way. An agreement on this basis was concluded by direct negotiations carried on at Geneva between German and Polish representatives under the auspices of the League, the decisions taken to run for fifteen years. An Upper Silesia Arbitral Tribunal was created to settle differences arising in that period. The system has, on the whole, fulfilled hopes and has unquestionably mitigated many of the hardships the enforced division of Upper Silesia must have involved. In the view of *The Times* correspondent in Upper Silesia, the League succeeded in making the new frontier " a line of union rather than of division." [1] Whatever the final judgment on that may be, the League scheme has a broad importance as foreshadowing the lines on which difficulties and discontents arising on various other post-war frontiers may be gradually removed.

(4) *The Jugoslav Threat to Albania.*—This dispute is important as being the only case in the first five years of the League's history in which Article XVI (" sanctions " or penalties) was directly invoked. The occasion was an invasion of Albanian territory in the autumn of 1921 by Jugoslav troops. The matter was brought before the Council (under Article XI of the Covenant) by the British Government, which asked the Council to consider what measures should be taken against Jugoslavia under Article XVI. The Council was immediately convened and met in Paris, Albanian and Jugoslav representatives being present. It was then found that the mere prospect of the imposition of sanctions was enough. It had resulted in an immediate depreciation of Jugoslav currency, and gravely compromised the hopes of an impending loan. The Jugoslav delegate, therefore, gave explicit pledges to respect

[1] *Five Years of European Chaos*, by Maxwell Macartney.

the frontier which the Conference of Ambassadors had just defined, and the Council appointed a commission (consisting of a Luxemburger, a Norwegian and a Finn) to make a prolonged stay in the disputed region and see that the pledge was carried out. No further trouble, in point of fact, arose.

(5) *The Memel Dispute.*—This illustrates one more type of League methods. The port of Memel on the Baltic, with a narrow strip of adjacent territory containing the mouth of the River Niemen (which serves Lithuania, Poland and to a small extent Russia) was taken from Germany by the Treaty of Versailles and retained in the hands of the Allies down to the middle of 1923. It was always intended to hand it over to Lithuania, which has no other outlet to the sea, but Poland made extensive claims regarding the use of the river and the port, and the predominantly German population of the territory had also to be considered. The Conference of Ambassadors, after long deliberations, drew up a statute which Lithuania flatly refused to consider, on the ground that it was far too favourable to Poland. A complete deadlock resulting, the matter was referred to the League as a dispute between the Allied Powers and Lithuania. Poland was not a direct party to the issue. The League Council at its meeting in December 1923 considered the problem, and taking the view that the dispute, though in some aspects political, turned largely on technical questions concerned with navigation of the river, decided to entrust investigation of the situation to a small commission consisting of two transit experts, a Swede

and a Dutchman, presided over by an impartial
political head, Mr. Norman Davis, a former
Acting Secretary of State in the United States.
The commissioners, getting rapidly to work,
produced a most able report embodying recom-
mended agreements regarding all the points at
issue, and this was accepted at the League Council
table by all the Allied representatives on the one
hand and the Lithuanian Prime Minister on the
other. The statute thus approved was shortly
afterwards put into operation.

Among other examples of disputes dealt with by
the Council may be mentioned particularly those
between Great Britain and France over military
service in Tunis and Morocco ; between Italy and
Greece over events arising out of the murder of the
Italian General Tellini on Greek soil ; and between
Great Britain and Turkey over the northern frontier
of Iraq. The Tunis-Morocco question was, as already
mentioned, referred to the Court of International
Justice and settled by agreement on the basis of the
Court's verdict.

The Corfu issue was complicated from the first by
the fact that although Greece appealed to the League
under Article XI, she simultaneously put herself
completely in the hands of the Conference of Ambassadors, in whose service the unfortunate Italian
general was at the time of his murder. As Italy also
accepted the jurisdiction of the Conference of Ambassadors, it became for all practical purposes an arbitral
tribunal such as is indicated in Article XIII of the
Covenant. The League Council, therefore, had no
ground for intervening actively, but it pursued its
study of the facts, exercised a valuable conciliatory

influence and forwarded to the Ambassadors a suggested plan of settlement, the chief features of which were actually adopted. It was the expressed view of the then British Prime Minister, Mr. Baldwin, that the Council's discreet action in this case averted a war of which there was grave danger.

The Iraq frontier question, referred to the League in accordance with certain provisions of the Treaty of Lausanne (between Great Britain and Turkey), was handled at two successive sessions, a second meeting having to be called owing to complaints that Turkey was violating what, it was claimed, was a provisional frontier line temporarily agreed on. Both sides consented to accept the Council's decision, and an expert commission, consisting of a Dutchman, a Swede and a Belgian, visited London, Angora and the disputed frontier itself in the winter of 1924-5, with a view to providing the Council with the detailed information necessary for its decision.

From these examples it will be seen that the Council, though it has by this time dealt with enough cases to provide various precedents for future action, is in no danger of following rule-of-thumb methods. Unlike a court of law, it has its hands entirely free and can and does adopt in each particular dispute whatever course seems best suited to the circumstances of the case. Such flexibility of procedure adds considerably to the Council's efficiency as an instrument of conciliation.

CHAPTER VII

THE ARMAMENTS PROBLEM

The League's Responsibility—The Armaments Committees—
Traffic in Arms—The Esher Proposal—Disarmament and
Security—Treaty of Mutual Assistance—Geneva Protocol
—Naval Disarmament.

THE reduction of armaments is an obligation on all
nations that signed the Treaty of Versailles, for the
Preamble to the Military Clauses of the Treaty
declared that Germany's disarmament was being
imposed on her " in order to render possible the
initiation of a general limitation of the armaments of
all nations." For the execution of this general disarmament agreement the League of Nations was made
responsible, Article VIII of the Covenant laying on
the League the duty of :

(1) Formulating plans for definite reduction.
(2) Considering how the evils attendant on the
    private manufacture of munitions can be
    prevented, and
(3) Arranging for the exchange of " full and frank
    information " between members of the League
    regarding their armaments, and such of their
    industries as are adaptable to war purposes.

It is within the field so defined that the League has
been moving during its first five years. Before con-

sidering the steps it has taken, the machinery by which it works may be examined. Article IX of the Covenant provided for the creation of a permanent commission to advise the Council on military matters. This body was brought into actual existence in 1920 under the name of the Permanent Advisory Committee, a term usually abbreviated to P.A.C. It consists of naval, military and air representatives of each of the ten States represented on the Council, and is served by a special section of the Secretariat. Side by side with it there worked till the date of the Fifth Assembly in 1924 another body known as the Temporary Mixed Commission on Armaments, commonly known in its turn as the T.M.C. The creation of the T.M.C. was due to recognition of the fact that the problem of disarmament raises many issues—economic, political and industrial—which lie well outside the purview of naval and military experts. The T.M.C. therefore was composed of six experts from the P.A.C., with whom were associated leading statesmen like M. Viviani for France and Lord Robert Cecil for Great Britain, together with leading economists and financial authorities, as well as respresentatives both of employers and of organized Labour. From the time of its inception early in 1922 down to the Fifth Assembly, when a new committee took its place, the T.M.C. did most valuable work, and was in fact responsible for every important step taken by the League in the field of disarmament.

Before discussing what may be termed the League's direct attacks on the main problem, it will be convenient to consider briefly certain subsidiary issues, some of which are more important than they seem. The compilation of statistics is a comparatively trivial matter in itself, but it is the natural and most effective method of giving effect to the undertaking regarding the exchange of full and frank information on armaments. In deciding on the publication of an Armament's Year Book, as complete as the information obtainable could make it, the League took no exaggerated views of the value of such a document, which could not by the nature of things contain such facts as every State does its utmost to keep secret. Even so, however, the first issue of the Year Book in 1924 did bring together in one volume fuller information about the armaments of the world than is obtainable elsewhere, and further developments are hoped for in subsequent years. It was believed by the T.M.C. that even this modest element of publicity would do something to check Press scares regarding the armaments of possibly hostile nations.

Much the most important part, however, of the secondary tasks of the T.M.C. has been the endeavour to secure international agreement regarding control of the private manufacture of arms, and the international traffic in munitions. Only the former of these was dealt with in Article VIII of the Covenant, for the good reason that the question of the international traffic was believed to have been disposed of by a convention which was in contemplation at Paris in 1919, and was actually signed at St. Germain in that year. Unfortunately this agreement, which provided for a general restraint by the Governments of all nations on those of its manufacturers who desired to send munitions abroad, was never ratified by the Great Powers, the obstacle being the United States, which declined to endorse any of the agreements entered into under President Wilson's direction during the Peace Conference. Since an agreement in which the United States had no part would merely mean throwing the arms trade throughout the world into the hands of the American manufacturers, the whole convention fell to the ground.

The League, therefore, had to deal with the question of the international traffic as well as with the question of private manufacture in each country, and when the T.M.C. got down to serious business, it found that the arms traffic had better be tackled first: Long delays were involved in unsuccessful attempts to persuade the American Government to explain first of all what it objected to in the St. Germain Convention, and secondly what kind of agreement it would be ready to approve. Gradually, however, the State Department in Washington modified its attitude, and by 1924 it was prepared to allow an American representative actually to sit with the T.M.C. and assist it in drafting a new convention. This task was accomplished in the summer of 1924, in time for the efforts of the T.M.C. to be approved by the Assembly of that year. America indicated her willingness to take part in an International Conference to be called by the League for the general adoption of the convention thus prepared, and such a conference was accordingly convened for May 1925. The main provisions of the convention prescribed the institution of a strict system of licences for arms exports from every country, and the exclusion of arms imports altogether from various undeveloped areas, including nearly the whole of Africa and extensive coastal regions in South-West Asia. Full information of all licences granted was to be filed at a central office under the control of the League. Concurrently with the drafting of this convention the T.M.C. was studying the question of the private manufacture of arms, and the preparation of a convention on that subject to be adopted similarly at an international conference was ordered by the Fifth Assembly in 1924.

But these are, after all, subsidiary phases of the disarmament problem. The endeavour to secure direct reduction or limitation of the world's armies and navies has been made by the League in other ways. The first attempt was interesting, but a little too simple and logical on paper to hold ground in an atmosphere where human emotions exert so strong a sway. It took the form of a proposal put forward in the T.M.C. by Lord Esher, who was then a member of that body, that the army and navy allotted to Germany under the Treaty of Versailles should be regarded broadly as the criterion of a nation's needs. If, it was argued, 100,000 men were enough for the defence of a country of such and such an area and with such and such a population, it was a matter of easy calculation to discover what armies and navies were necessary for other countries with different area and population. That being so, a scheme was put forward according to which each nation was to be allotted an army consisting of a certain number of units each representing 30,000 men, with, of course, the appropriate equipment. France, for example, was to have six such units, Great Britain three, Norway two, Poland four, and so on, some allowance being made for special dangers to which any individual country might be considered to be exposed. The scheme was ingenious, but it never looked like gaining acceptance and was soon allowed to drop.

After other minor advances towards a solution of the problem, notably the adoption by the Assembly in two successive years of a resolution, which was by no means without effect, urging all nations to limit their Budget expenditure on armaments to the figure of the preceding year, the League applied itself to its task in fresh earnest at the Assembly of 1922. In that year, after a series of notable discussions between Lord Robert Cecil (who was then representing South Africa and had his hands comparatively free) and the French delegate, M. Henry de Jouvenel, a resolution was adopted which has formed the starting-point of all subsequent discussions. Its essential feature was that it recognized the dominant fact in the military situation in Europe, the imperative demand of a number of continental nations for security, and a security based definitely on military assurance. Known historically as Resolution XIV of the Third Assembly, this statement of foundation principles opens with the declaration that " no scheme for the reduction of armaments can be fully successful unless it is general," and adds that

" in the present state of the world many Governments would be unable to accept the responsibility for a successful reduction of armaments unless they received in exchange a satisfactory guarantee of the safety of their country."

Such a guarantee, it was asserted, could be found in a defensive agreement which should be open to all countries, binding them to provide immediate and effective assistance in accordance with a pre-arranged plan in the event of one of them being attacked.

This resolution was the origin of the Draft Treaty of Mutual Assistance, of which much was heard in the years 1923 and 1924. The principle of the treaty was simple and by no means new. As a matter of fact, though no one at Geneva seemed to remember it, the treaty had been definitely foreshadowed by President Wilson in June 1918 in a speech to Mexican editors, in which he launched the idea of a general

American guarantee extending later to the whole world. The aim of the actual Treaty of Mutual Guarantee could not be more tersely expressed than in Mr. Wilson's informal invitation, " Let us agree that if any one of us, the United States included, violates the political independence or territorial in- tegrity of any of the others, all the others will jump on her," and the President indicated that he regarded this as merely a first step by adding, " that is the kind of agreement that will have to be the foundation of the future life of the nations of the world. The whole family of nations will have to guarantee to each nation that no nation shall violate its political independence or its territorial integrity."

A treaty embodying these principles, but bringing them into direct touch with the disarmament problem by laying it down that no nation should be entitled to claim protection under the treaty unless it had already reduced (or was in process of reducing) its armaments to a level approved by the League Council, was framed by the T.M.C. and by it presented to the Fourth Assembly (1923) which ordered it to be laid before the respective Governments, including those of countries outside the League, for their observations. The full details of the treaty are not relevant here, for it was abandoned, largely as the result of British opposition, at the Assembly of 1924. What it provided, briefly, was that a nation which attacked another should be regarded as a common enemy and be exposed to economic and, if necessary, military pressure by every member of the League ; that the often difficult question of who was the actual aggressor should be decided by the League Council ; that separate agreements between groups of States for mutual help should be permitted within the framework of the general agreement; and that (as already stated) no nation should be entitled to claim protection under the treaty unless it had disarmed or was disarming. Security was to be conferred in order to make disarmament possible, and unless disarmament did take place the guarantee of security would lapse.

Discussion of the treaty, which France and other Continental nations welcomed, did a good deal to clarify ideas during 1924, but in July of that year the British Labour Government, which feared that certain States might develop provocative policies under cover of the protection they believed the treaty would give them, pronounced against it. Discussions at the Fifth Assembly in September 1924 had, therefore, to take a different turn. They forsook rather the form than the principles of the Treaty of Mutual Assistance and took shape before the Assembly rose in the document known as the Geneva Protocol. The aim of the Protocol was to eliminate the risk of the League being called on to defend a State whose cause was manifestly unjust. Governments of the Left in Great Britain and France thought the time had come when the peaceful settlement of all disputes could be insisted on and the provisions of the Covenant extended to secure the acceptance of some form of arbitral verdict on every kind of difference between nations (except those arising from matters found to fall within a particular country's jurisdiction). An agreement to that end was therefore grafted on, or rather prefixed, to the provisions of the Treaty of Mutual Assistance regarding guarantees of security. Under the Protocol every State undertakes to submit to arbitration any dispute in which it may be engaged, and to accept the verdict given, all agreeing equally to regard as a common enemy a State which takes up arms rather than submit to arbitration or comply with the verdict given. Economic, and if need be military, action is to be taken by all members of the League against a State so offending.

These are the essential features of the Protocol, which was only to take effect after a Disarmament Conference of all nations, to be summoned by the League, had adopted some practicable scheme for the general reduction of armaments. The security and disarmament issues are thus interlocked under the Protocol as they were under the Treaty of Mutual Assistance. Though the Protocol was put by its authors at the Fifth Assembly in what was intended to be final form, and immediate signature and ratification was invited, the change of Government which took place immediately afterwards in Great Britain made it clear that the best to be hoped was that the document should be regarded, like the Treaty of Mutual Assistance, as a draft, susceptible of fresh discussion and amendment at the Assembly of 1925. It will be noted that the Protocol embodies the principle, increasingly popular in America, of the complete outlawry of all war between individual nations.

Such was the point reached by the League's disarmament endeavours by the end of 1924. Naval disarmament had been largely left aside, owing to the fact that the Washington Conference of 1921–2 had done all that seemed possible in the way of an agreement between the chief naval States of the world. The League did, however, contemplate extending the principles of that agreement to States not represented at Washington, and a conference of experts to prepare the ground for a conference to secure that was held at Rome early in 1924. The progress made was disappointing and the matter reverted to the Assembly. By the time the Assembly met, a general disarmament conference in connection with the Protocol was being projected, and the proposed naval meeting was therefore left to merge itself in the larger gathering. Chemical warfare has also been faced by the League, which found, like the Washington Conference, that no effective means of limiting it seem possible. The Assembly therefore confined itself to publishing, in 1924, a report, based on memoranda supplied by the leading chemists and bacteriologists of all countries, giving some indication of what the horrors of chemical war in the future might be, it being held that the public, which in the last resort is responsible for war and peace policies, ought to understand clearly what war now means.

CHAPTER VIII

RECONSTRUCTING EUROPE

The Austrian Scheme—League Supervision—International Loan—Austria's Part—Hungarian Reconstruction—Greek Refugee Scheme.

THE series of tasks in which the League has perhaps attained more success than in any other field fell to it as it were by chance. It would be difficult to point to any article of the Covenant or of the post-war Treaties which covered the enterprises for which the League made itself responsible in the years 1922-4, in connection with the economic reconstruction of Austria and Hungary, and the floating of the Refugee Settlement Scheme in Greece. That this was, in a sense, prosaic and material work, initiated and carried out in the main through the League's Economic and Financial Organization, is true enough, but it had, in point of fact, a high human and political value, particularly in the case of the Austrian scheme, the first, and in many ways the most difficult, of the League's undertakings.

The story of Austria down to the date in the autumn of 1922, when the League's scheme was drafted, is quickly told. The provisions of the Peace Treaty with Austria may have been inevitable, but they were fatal to the country's economic life. Vienna, once the capital of an empire of over 50,000,000 people, remained still the capital of a little shorn territory of some 6,000,000, and to it had flocked back, as their national headquarters, the tens of thousands of officials of one kind and another who had held posts under the old Austro-Hungarian Empire before the war. Out of a total population of 6,000,000, there were, in fact, 2,000,000 actually living in Vienna in 1922.

It seemed to sober observers that Austria could not survive as an economic unit, and through 1921 and most of the following year every indication lent colour to that belief. Taxes could not be raised ; the Budget consequently could not be balanced ; the currency consequently was debased, because the Government printed paper wildly to pay its swollen army of officials. The crown, from 24 to the pound, rose to the then unprecedented figure of 330,000. Bankruptcy seemed to be staring the country in the face, and the situation became the more desperate, in that Austria was in the position of a debtor owing, in the form of reparations to the victorious nations, vast sums which she had no possibility of paying. Those obligations formed a prior charge on all Austrian assets, so that there could be no prospect of raising fresh loans.

Certain charitable advances were indeed made, by the United States, in the form of food credits, and by Great Britain and other countries in actual money. This, however, simply enabled Austria to live from hand to mouth, and did nothing whatever to arrest her financial dissolution. At the beginning of 1921 the Allies, who felt some responsibility for the situation, invited the League to investigate it. A competent commission was accordingly sent to Vienna and a comprehensive report, with proposed remedies, drafted.

There were, however, fatal obstacles, since, as already pointed out, no one would lend Austria money so long as the Allied Powers and other earlier creditors had the first claim on all her resources. An attempt was consequently made to persuade the Allies, through the Reparation Commission, to waive their rights for twenty years. This was ultimately done, but it took time. It took still longer time to get the United States to stand aside for the same period, and there still remained Austria's immediate neighbours, in a region of Europe where suspicions and hostilities died hard, with claims they were by no means disposed to relinquish. Austria, as a consequence, drifted steadily and with increasing momentum towards complete disaster.

That continued till August of 1922, when the Supreme Council of the Allies happened to be meeting in London to discuss German Reparations, and Dr. Seipel, the curiously picturesque Prelate-Premier of Austria, addressed a despairing appeal to the statesmen gathered in Downing Street. Little attention could be spared for Austria. A short and cursory conversation took place, and as a result the League was requested to look into the matter at once, and " gather further information," a discouraging warning being added that no more money could be found for Austria unless it could be raised through loans in the open market in the ordinary way. That seemed another way of extinguishing Austria's last hopes, for bankrupts cannot borrow, and Austria was to all intents and purposes a bankrupt.

Under such conditions the League might well have declined the task thrust upon it. It decided, however, to try its hand. The Assembly was about to meet at Geneva, and during the Assembly the Council was in more or less constant session. The chief executive instrument of the League dealt at once with the Allied request, constituting a special committee, under the chairmanship of Lord Balfour, and including in its number Dr. Benès, then Prime Minister of Czechoslovakia, as representing those neighbours of Austria hostile to her in the war whose claims on her remained still unsatisfied. The disease had been, more or less, diagnosed by the League's Financial and Economic Commission, and proposals regarding the remedy had taken specific shape. The question remained to decide whether they were practical propositions, and if so to endeavour to apply them.

This was no easy matter, as more than mere financial questions were involved. Political considerations, some of them obvious enough, others springing from motives at first carefully concealed, complicated matters at every turn. The outlines of the problem, however, were reasonably clear. Austria had to have money to carry on with till she could set her affairs in order, and she could only get it in the form of an external loan. On the other hand, till she had set her affairs in order no one was likely to lend her money. From that vicious circle there was no possible escape.

The League, however, developed its scheme. The first obstacles to clear from the way were those claims on Austria still outstanding. Persuasion at Geneva effected that. Austria, as a result, was given twenty years' respite in which to raise the new loan and pay it back, before her old creditors came besetting her once more. But there was no one who would lend money to a Government without strength of mind or political experience to spend it wisely. The League dealt with that obstacle by arranging that the proceeds of the loan, if one could be arranged, should be handed over, not direct to the Austrian Government, but to a League High Commissioner established at Vienna, who would disburse it month by month only so long as he was satisfied that Austria was faithfully carrying out the scheme of financial reforms prepared by the League.

That scheme provided for the gradual increase of taxation and reduction of expenditure, for the immediate and absolute abandonment of the hopeless expedient of printing more and more fresh money, for the gradual dismissal of a large number of the vast army of now useless officials and railway servants still figuring on the Government pay-roll. Of these 100,000 were to be dismissed in two years, and within the same period the budget was to be balanced by increasing revenues and reducing expenditure. Even that was hardly likely in itself to produce a loan, and the League therefore advanced a proposal whose acceptance at first seemed somewhat doubtful. This was that certain Allied Governments, in particular those of Great Britain, France and Italy, should actually guarantee the capital and interest of the proposed loan, the total of which was rather over £26,000,000. After critical negotiations, the Governments gave their consent. But one equally important question still remained. Would Austria accept the strict financial control considered necessary, or would she, as would have been natural enough, discover interested motives in the action of her former enemies, and suspect an endeavour on their part to secure through the loan a definite political or financial hold on her country ? This objection again the League removed effectively, for it secured the signature at Geneva of a formal protocol, whereby the countries concerned bound themselves during the period of the currency of the loan to seek no territorial advantage or economic privilege at Austria's expense, Austria, on her part, binding herself, by the same instrument, neither to confer any such privilege, nor to alienate any of her territory.

On that basis the scheme was adopted in October 1922. On the day the Committee first met, the Austrian Chancellor, speaking in German in the Council Room at Geneva, declared that : " the Austrian people, rather than perish in its isolation, will make an utmost final effort to break the bonds which imprison and strangle it. It is for the League of Nations to see that this is done without the peace of the world being disturbed." A month later, Dr. Seipel, who had himself sat as a member of the Committee throughout, again addressed it. He referred to his earlier doubts and misgivings, " but," he continued, " thank God we can say to-day the League of Nations has not failed us."

In all essentials the Austrian scheme has fully justified the hopes of its authors. Its immediate results, indeed, were remarkable. The loan of 650,000,000 gold crowns, backed as it was by the guarantee of the Allied Governments, was immediately over-subscribed in London, New York and other centres. The League secured as its High Commissioner Dr. Zimmerman, who had for many years been Burgomaster of Rotterdam, and the Austrian Government on its side carried without difficulty the legislation embodying the administrative reforms required under the League scheme.

From the moment, moreover, when the discussions at Geneva began to take serious shape, the Austrian crown, which had been depreciating with increasing

rapidity, ceased its movement and remained completely stable at the then figure of 330,000 to the
pound. It would have, of course, been easy to improve
on that figure. It was, indeed, difficult sometimes
not to do so. But what trade required was a fixed
currency rather than one fluctuating in either direction,
and 330,000 was therefore tacitly accepted as the new
and standard relationship of the crown to the pound.
Simultaneously deposits in the Savings Banks began
steadily to increase, an unfailing sign of revived
confidence, for it would obviously have been useless
to lay-by money when there was every probability
that before it could be drawn out again its value
would have gone down by 25 or 50 per cent. Now,
with money remaining stable, normal habits of thrift
were resumed.

The working-out of the Austrian scheme has,
naturally, not been free from all difficulty. The
scheme itself was based on the best estimate an expert
League Commission could make. No special sanctity,
however, attached to their views, as members of the
Commission themselves would be the first to recognize,
and some modifications had later to be made. In
particular, the programme of the dismissal of 100,000
State officials in two years was not fully realized.
Necessary though the measure was, it was naturally
enough unpopular and difficult for any Government to
carry through, and the Austrian Government, like all
others, has political opponents ready enough to make
capital out of its difficulties. About 70,000 were
actually dismissed in the two-year period. Some
change had also to be made in the Budget total. It
was at first thought that Austria's running expenses
could be met by a Budget total of 350,000,000 gold
crowns. This proved in working to be too low, and

on the urgent insistence of the Austrian Government the League Council in September 1924 sanctioned an increase to 495,000,000, stipulating at the same time that some changes be made in financial methods, for Austria, in a certain excess of zeal, had been balancing her Budget prematurely through quite excessive taxation.

All things considered, both the League and Austria have had abundant reason to be satisfied with the progress of the first great reconstruction scheme planned at Geneva. In the opening speech at the Fourth Assembly of 1923, Viscount Ishii declared that " the most notable single achievement of the League during the past year has been the work of reconstruction in Austria." Since then similar pieces of work have been undertaken in Hungary and Greece, but nothing has happened to detract from the implied tribute thus paid by the Japanese delegate to the authors of the Austrian scheme. That scheme was, in a sense, primarily economic, but its political and social effects were far reaching. It kept industry and employment alive in a country fast drifting into dissolution, and it maintained in existence a political unit, the disappearance of which might have sent three or four neighbouring States rushing in to fill a vacuum, at the risk of a collision calculated to precipitate a new European War.

Less need be said about the Hungarian and Greek schemes, not because they are less intrinsically important than the Austrian, but because they were based largely on principles already explained in connection with the League's pioneer enterprise in this field. Hungary, in 1923, applied spontaneously to the League for the kind of assistance already accorded to Austria. Her problem was economically simpler, for her currency had not depreciated quite so far, and the fact that the country depended much more largely on agriculture gave her a stability her neighbour did no enjoy.

On the other hand, the political complications were greater, for Hungary had been none too scrupulous in the observance of her Treaty obligations, and her neighbours, particularly the little Entente States of Czechoslovakia, Jugoslavia and Rumania, regarded her with not unjustified suspicions. They were, therefore, extremely reluctant to abandon any of their reparation claims on her, an operation which, as in Austria's case, was essential before any external loan could be floated. Gradually, however, the difficulties were straightened out, and a scheme largely similar to that already at work in Austria was approved by the League Council and accepted by the Hungarian Government. An able American lawyer, Mr. Jeremiah Smith of Boston, was appointed High Commissioner of the League, like Dr. Zimmerman at Vienna, to see that the League programme of financial reform was duly carried out, and authorized to disburse the proceeds of the loan on that condition only. In both countries the loan was secured on certain State revenues especially set aside for the purpose. These have proved fully sufficient for all needs.

An important feature of the Hungarian scheme was its demonstration of the value in the money-market of a League guarantee of wise expenditure. Not only could no outside States be found to guarantee the Hungarian loan as they had the Austrian, but in addition, while Austria was relieved of all reparation payments for twenty years, Hungary still remained liable to a limited extent to the Reparation Commission. In spite of these drawbacks, the mere fact that the League, which had already demonstrated its efficiency in the case of Austria, was prepared to be answerable for the soundness of Hungarian expenditure during the currency of the loan, secured the issue in the London and American markets an even more striking success than the Austrian had achieved. At the end of 1924 the Hungarian scheme, which had then been in operation a little over six months, was working with apparently unqualified success.

While the League Council had been thrashing out details of the Hungarian plan, it was equally deeply engaged on a reconstruction scheme for Greece. There a quite different problem was presented. The country as a whole was solvent, but a situation had arisen with which it could not cope, through the influx into its territories of something over 1,000,000 refugees of Greek origin and race, who fled from Asia Minor and Eastern Thrace when the Turkish armies finally threw the Greeks back across the Aegean at the end of 1922. This unhappy mass of fugitives poured into Greece destitute of everything except the tattered rags of clothing they wore. They had no money, no beasts, no furniture, no tools. For a while they subsisted on charity, the Greek Government advancing what money it could, and the League doing what lay in its power to administer relief through Dr. Nansen, and to fight disease in the congested camps through its Health Organization. But these were, of course, only temporary measures. Fortunately the problem was not in itself insoluble. The refugees were capable of work if money could be found to drain and fence land, to provide them with tools and cattle and seed corn, or to set them up in some industry in the towns. Given a carefully framed scheme, this, in the view of the League Commission which investigated conditions on the spot, was a business proposition, and there was no reason why money lent them for this purpose should not in due course be repaid with interest, and Greece itself be made in the end the more prosperous through the increase of its productive output.

A League plan was framed on these lines, and accepted with full appreciation by the Greek Government. The scheme was to be administered by a committee of four, two of them representing the Greek Government, and two the League, one of the League nominees being Chairman, with the right of exercising a casting vote in case of need. The first Chairman to be appointed was Mr. Henry Morgenthau, formerly American Ambassador at Constantinople, and when he had to return to America in the latter part of 1924, his place was taken by a fellow American, Mr. Charles P. Howland of New York. The unsettled political situation in Greece made the floating of the loan difficult in the early part of 1924, and through that period the work was financed on advances by the Greek Government and two short-term loans from the Bank of England. When, however, the long-term loan was floated in November, it achieved an instantaneous and overwhelming success, applications for the London section of the loan totalling more than twenty times the amount needed.

Everything therefore at the end of 1924 promised well for the Greek scheme, as for the Austrian and Hungarian. Here again it would be a mistake to regard the enterprise as purely economic. The political unsettlement that might result from the influx into a country with a population of 5,000,000 of over a million refugees was a possibility Europe could not regard with equanimity, particularly when so perilous a region as the Balkans was concerned. All three schemes, therefore, fall properly within that opening clause of the Preamble of the Covenant where the League is declared to exist " to promote international co-operation and achieve international peace and security."

CHAPTER IX

THE LEAGUE'S BUSINESS SIDE

The Economic and Financial Organization—The Brussels
Financial Conference—Studies in Taxation—The Customs
Conference—Communications and Transit—Barcelona
Conference—Transit Convention—The Railways and Ports
Convention—The Reform of the Calendar.

IT˙ has already been explained that while all the
League's business goes through the hands of the
Assembly and of the Council or both, the latter body,
consisting as it does of ten individuals whose experience
lies mainly in the diplomatic sphere, has built up
round itself a series of expert committees, whose
advice it consistently follows, and whose schemes it
adopts, within the field of the particular committee's
operations. One set of such committees deals mainly
with what may be termed social and humanitarian
work. Another, comprising what are known as the
League's " technical organizations," handles mainly
those questions arising out of the endeavour to simplify
international relations in regard to commercial transactions and the transport of goods, or to improve them
in the field of health and sanitation. The three
principal technical organizations are, thus, the Economic and Financial, the Communications and Transit,
and the Health. If the two former appear at first
sight to deal with questions of a somewhat restricted
interest, it is necessary to remember that they give

6

the League a status of its own in the vastly important world of business, and they have, in point of fact, effected within that field reforms the value of which has been generally recognized.

The main achievements of the Economic and Financial Organization have indeed already been discussed, for it is this body which, subject of course to the general authority of the League Council, has been responsible for the successful formulation and working of the three reconstruction schemes in Austria, Hungary and Greece. On these nothing more need be said. The Economic and Financial Organization, which consists of two separate committees, one economic and one financial, which from time to time hold joint meetings, has been applying itself to a number of those unsolved problems the existence of which does much to hinder the smooth flow of commercial intercourse between different countries. In this field the League has been singularly fortunate in securing the voluntary services, as members of one or other committee, of some of the foremost economists and financiers in Europe. Some of them, like Sir Otto Niemeyer, Controller of Finance in the British Treasury, are high Government officials; others, like M. ter Meulen, head of a well-known Dutch house, or M. Marcus Wallenberg of Sweden, bankers of international reputation; others like Signor Pirelli, maker of the well-known pneumatic tyre, business men known throughout Europe and beyond. Thanks to their ready assistance and their willingness to devote considerable time to the meetings of the committees, the Economic and Financial Organization can claim to be as effective an instrument as any organ connected with the League. It had the distinction also of being responsible for the first great international gathering convened under the League's auspices. This was the Brussels Financial Conference held in September 1920, three months before the First Assembly. The object of the Conference, which was attended by representatives of thirty-nine States, including the U.S.A. and Germany, was not to draft an international convention but rather to seek some agreement on immediate problems which might guide Governments, particularly of new States, through the financial chaos in which Europe was then submerged. In that the Conference was entirely successful. It was prepared for by the publication of a series of important monographs on various financial questions by leading authorities in different countries, and its unanimously approved report has ever since formed a kind of standard by which national budgets can be tested. The fact that a country so rigorously prudent in its finance as Great Britain is may not have much to learn from the Brussels resolutions must not obscure their far-reaching importance as a stimulus to those Governments, representing practically every country in Europe, which were then failing hopelessly to balance their annual budgets.

In addition to the responsibility it bears for the preparation of the Austrian, Hungarian and Greek schemes, the Economic and Financial Organization took a leading part in drafting the economic section of the Upper Silesian agreement : it carried through a scheme for the reconstruction of the finances of Danzig ; and in 1923 it found a financial advisor for the Albanian Government to assist in the financial administration of the country at the Government's request. It has, in addition, been steadily pursuing investigations into various secondary problems important to practically every State member of the

League. Notable among these are the questions of
" double taxation " and " fiscal evasion." Double
taxation means the liability of a taxpayer in one
country and holding investments in another to be
taxed by the Governments of both. Fiscal evasion
means, such devices as the export of capital, with the
intention, sometimes successful, of evading taxation
altogether. But neither of these investigations has
yet arrived at a stage on which international conventions on the subject can be signed. That stage
has, however, been reached in connection with one
important section of the Organization's activities, the
inquiry into the simplification of Customs formalities.
A conference was called on this subject by the League
at the end of 1923 and attended by representatives
of thirty-five States, under the chairmanship of Earl
Buxton. An important convention was unanimously
adopted providing, briefly, for the removal of grievances
regarding Customs formalities both as regards travellers
and as regards goods (the latter of course being much
the more important) by providing for publicity of
regulations, simplicity in procedure, expedition in
handling, equality of treatment and facilities for
redress.

The conference formed one method of carrying out
the League's obligations under that clause of
Article XXIII of the Covenant which charges it with
" securing and maintaining equitable treatment " for
the commerce of all members of the League. The
Organization is further discharging the same duty by
endeavouring to make provision by international
agreement against false trade-marks and descriptions,
unfair discrimination against foreign nationals admitted to the territory of another State and unjust
discrimination against the commerce of any one single

State. One minor agreement negotiated by the Organization, and to which much importance is attached in British business circles, provides for the recognition by the Courts of all signatory States of arbitration clauses in commercial contracts. Altogether the Economic and Financial Organization can claim credit for a highly satisfactory record of systematic work, resulting in the gradual removal of a number of obstacles which hinder the free flow of trade between country and country. The declaration of a particularly high authority in the British business world that the Customs Conference at Geneva had done more in a month than could have been achieved in fifty years by the old method of diplomatic negotiations may be an exaggeration, it serves none the less as a striking example of the impression made by the methods pursued at Geneva in this field on disinterested observers well qualified to judge.

The second of the League's main technical organizations, that dealing with communications and transit, was created to assist the Council in carrying out the provisions of Article XXIII of the Covenant regarding "freedom of communications and of transit for all members of the League." The importance of such a task, though the work of the Organization is by no means confined to Europe, is demonstrated by the most cursory glance at any map of the Europe of to-day. A political settlement which changed frontiers, broke up great Empires into small States, and cut off some of them from access to the sea, made it essential that every State should fully recognize every other's just rights in the matter of transit unless the commercial and industrial life of the Continent was to be hopelessly impeded. The political controversies which have arisen over the use of such ports as Danzig and Memel and Fiume, and to a lesser extent Salonica and Dedeagatch, shows the importance attaching to agreements such as the Transit Organization has been able to effect through its international convention on the use of ports generally. The manifest necessity of equal freedom of navigation for all States touching great rivers like the Rhine and the Danube, the Elbe and the Vistula, as well as many others in Europe, Asia, Africa and America, demonstrates equally the value of the convention on navigable waterways concluded at the Transit Organization's first general conference at Barcelona in 1921. Generally speaking the principle laid down and applied as the different circumstances of each case require is that of fair treatment for everyone concerned. In the case of rivers, for example, it is provided that every State controlling a stretch of the waterway must allow its free use to every State interested, and must maintain its waterways in a proper navigable condition through dredging and lighthouses, buoys, etc., so far as may be necessary. In the case of ports there is similarly to be equal treatment for all comers in such matters as tariffs, dues, regulations, use of warehouses, etc., a definite guarantee being given by signatories of the convention that there shall be no discrimination against the shipping of any one particular State and no special favour even for the nationals of the State in which the port is situated. In the case of railways (an International Railway Convention was signed at the second general Transit Conference at Geneva in 1923) the difficulties in the way of through travelling are to be smoothed away as far as possible by the simplification of formalities at frontiers, by the interchange of rolling stock between different States, by single through tickets for passengers, through registration of luggage and single through contract-notes for goods. In the same way the Transit Organization has done much, and still intends to do more, for the simplification of passports. Various duties are allotted to it under the different Peace Treaties, and in particular it is provided in a number of international agreements that any dispute arising out of the agreement shall go in the last resort to the Permanent Court of International Justice, but shall be referred first of all to the League Transit Committee for its mediation or arbitration.

One minor but interesting activity of the Transit Committee has been the appointment of a sub-committee on the reform of the Calendar, charged with considering the possibility, in particular, of arranging for a fixed instead of a movable Easter, and for a year which shall consist of an exact number of weeks instead of fifty-two weeks and one or two odd days. The committee was appointed at the desire of business men on purely business grounds, but it, of course, raised important ecclesiastical questions, and its membership therefore consists rather curiously of authorities on transit and law and business generally, sitting side by side with representatives of the Vatican, the Archbishop of Canterbury and the Eastern Orthodox Church. This is only one of a whole system of sub-committees to which the main Transit Committee has delegated the examination of special technical questions.

The Organization may now be regarded as complete, and its efficiency in redressing, though it has by no means yet succeeded in eliminating, the obstacles to the free movement of trade across whole Continents is generally recognized. Incidentally also it has provided an example of the value of collaboration between different League organisms by its co-operation with the Opium Committee in considering measures for the suppression of opium smuggling in free ports, and with the Health Organization in discussing the question of river-borne and sea-borne disease

CHAPTER X

THE WORLD'S HEALTH

The Health Organization—The Fight against Typhus—The Epidemics Commission—International Conventions—Warsaw Conference.

No League agency is more valuable, and none has succeeded in attaining more important results on slender resources, than the Health Organization, brought into existence to carry out the duty imposed on the League in the last clause of Article XXIII of the Covenant, "to take steps in matters of international concern for the prevention and control of disease." The Health Organization consists to-day, like the League itself and the other technical organizations, of a threefold mechanism—the Health Advisory Council, the Health Committee and the Health section of the Secretariat. As in other cases, the main work is done by the committee, the results of its labours being reported to, and usually approved by, the larger advisory council.

It is manifest that the main business of the Health Organization must be to co-ordinate and give direction to national effort. It neither possesses nor has any prospect of obtaining funds or personnel to enable it to undertake large activities itself, nor would such assumption by an international body of duties belonging properly to national administrations be of permanent advantage. In spite of that the first main activity of the Health Organization, even before it had taken final form itself, was the organization of and active participation in a great campaign against typhus and other epidemics in Eastern Europe. The danger threatening the whole Continent through the eastward spread of disease shortly after the war came before the First Assembly of the League in December 1920, and a fund of some £200,000 was there and then raised from voluntary contributions by Governments to enable the Health Organization to take in hand work which the not very competent States in Eastern Europe found beyond their individual means. Even so, though the Health Organization equipped hospitals, supplied drugs and doctors, and took other direct action itself, the main value of its effort was the instruction and direction it gave to the administrations of the countries concerned, and the permanent measures it initiated for the prevention and control of disease in Eastern Europe. It was largely as a result of what was done at this time in Poland and Russia that the Soviet Government has consistently maintained with the Health Committee relations it has refused with any other League organ. While Russia, unlike Germany and the United States, has no permanent representative on the Health Committee, it sends a delegate when matters of special interest to Russia are discussed, it encourages its doctors to take part in the Committee's periodical interchanges of medical officials, it has welcomed a League commission on malaria to Russia, and it took an active part in the Health Conference arranged by the Health Organization at Warsaw in 1922. Altogether, therefore, the Health Organization has shown itself capable of overcoming obstacles due to national prejudices as well as to national frontiers.

A further point of interest about the Organization is that it is the first body associated with the League to establish a permanent branch outside Europe. The Epidemics Commission, which was created as part of the Health Organization to deal in the first instance with disease in Eastern Europe, has survived in spite of the intention that it should be only temporary, and in 1924 established an Office at Singapore (where a Health Conference for Far Eastern countries was held early in 1925) to direct the fight against disease in the Far East, much as it is directed for Europe from Geneva. Broadly speaking, what the Health Organization aims at is to place so far as possible the knowledge and experience acquired by each country at the disposal of all. By this co-ordination investigations and experiments can be undertaken for the world once for all instead of having to be carried on separately and simultaneously in a dozen different countries. The importance of international standards in health matters is great. It is essential that when doctors in different countries are using the same medical terms it should be certain that they are speaking about the same things. In such matters, for example, as sera that has been very far from certain. The League Health Organization therefore, after experiments conducted by scientists from a number of different countries in Denmark, has agreed on certain standards, for the maintenance of which the State Laboratory at Copenhagen has been made responsible.

Vital statistics are another matter to which the Committee has been giving attention. Apart from its day-to-day work of collecting and publishing health statistics from all quarters, with the conclusions to be drawn from them, it has conducted inquiries into such questions as statistical methods in regard to cancer in different countries. Cancer, indeed, is only one of a number of diseases into which the Committee has been pursuing its inquiries. Others are malaria, sleeping-sickness and tuberculosis, the study of malarial conditions having been particularly exhaustive.

Two other pieces of work call for special mention. One is the important system of interchange of public health officials which the Committee has been able to arrange through funds placed at its disposal by the Rockefeller Foundation of America. This consists in organizing parties of from twenty to thirty doctors from almost as many different countries, nominated usually by the medical associations in those countries, and arranging for them a two or three months' course of study of the health administration in some one country selected for the purpose. Such courses have been held in Great Britain and Belgium, Italy and the United States and elsewhere, the fullest facilities being given to the doctors by the country concerned for investigation into every aspect of its public health system.

To revert to more immediately practical work, the Health Committee organized in 1922-3 the inoculation against typhus and other diseases of over half a million refugees who had poured into Greece from Asia Minor after the final defeat of the Greek army by the Turkish army. It has assisted various inexperienced countries such as Persia and Albania by sending at their request members of its staff to organize medical services, and it has given advice to Turkey on the establishment of a Ministry of Health. More important still, perhaps, is the system of sanitary conventions concluded largely as a result of the Warsaw Health Conference between different nations in the East of Europe. It is clear that disease near a frontier must be met by preventive measures on both sides of the frontier if its spread is to be effectively averted. Where small countries are concerned, they can only fight disease successfully by fighting it together, and by encouraging the adoption of uniform methods and regular co-operation between Eastern European countries the League has done much to preserve that region from far worse epidemics than have actually ravaged it. A country where medical science is so far developed as it is in Great Britain has naturally less to learn from the League Health Organization than some others less advanced, but there is force in the observation of a leading British medical authority that by its important series of international experiments and inquiries the Health Organization has relieved this country of work it would otherwise have had to do for itself at an expense quite disproportionate to the trivial sum which represents that part of Great Britain's League contribution devoted to the League's health work.

CHAPTER XI

HUMANITARIAN EFFORT

Repatriation of Prisoners—Relief of Refugees—Opium Problem—Women and Children—Slavery—Intellectual Cooperation.

A NUMBER of interesting, if secondary, activities of the League are commonly grouped under the general head of Humanitarian Work. Most of them are conducted on the same basis as the technical organizations, in that the work is carried on by special advisory committees served by corresponding sections of the Secretariat and subject, of course, throughout to the League Council. The principal committees working in this sphere are those on the control of the opium traffic, on slavery, on the welfare of women and children, and on the suppression of obscene literature, while the general category of humanitarian work includes also the varied and beneficent labours of Dr. Nansen on behalf of prisoners of war, Russian refugees and other unfortunate classes of people to whom the League, through the agency of the Norwegian scientist, has been able to extend a helping hand.

It may be convenient to deal with Dr. Nansen's work first. The League, incidentally, has in a rather curious way converted the well-known Arctic explorer into a great humanitarian agent. The first task he undertook as League High Commissioner was the repatriation of some hundreds of thousands of prisoners of war who for one reason or another had been left stranded at vast distances from their homes, with little visible prospect of returning to them. This matter was brought before the League, and at its First Assembly Dr. Nansen was invited to study the question of repatriation and take what steps seemed possible. He set energetically to work, various Governments, including the British, providing funds for the purpose. The prisoners were of many nationalities. There were Russians still in Germany, there were Germans, Czechoslovakians and others still in parts of Russia as far distant as Eastern Siberia. Transport was a serious difficulty, for at that moment there was a tremendous demand for tonnage from all countries, and some contingents of prisoners had to be shipped back from as far afield as Vladivostock. Under these circumstances the completeness and the expedition with which the work was carried through reflected the highest credit on Dr. Nansen, and through him on the League. It was, moreover, executed with remarkable economy, for altogether 427,886 prisoners (many of whom had to be clothed before they could be moved) were restored to their homes by Dr. Nansen at a total cost of something under £400,000.

Dr. Nansen's success, indeed, marked him out as the League's indispensable agent when any task of this character presented itself. It was to him, accordingly, that the League turned in 1922 when there was laid before it the unhappy case of some 150,000 Russian refugees, hostile to the Soviet Government, who had had to fly from Russia after the final defeat of General Wrangel. Neither the repatriation of prisoners nor the relief of refugees directly concerned the League, but when the need was laid before it the

Assembly felt that some action must at least be attempted. Dr. Nansen accordingly took the refugee question in hand. Here, however, funds were a grave difficulty. The French Government agreed to continue certain help it was already giving to refugees at Constantinople, and the British Government provided £10,000 on condition another £20,000 was raised elsewhere to deal with one specific part of the problem. With these means at his disposal, Dr. Nansen was able to do much to relieve suffering. But perhaps his most important achievement was to secure the approval by some thirty Governments of identification certificates issued by his Organization to the refugees. These certificates were recognized by the Governments in question as equivalent to passports, for the great disability under which the refugees suffered was the fact that having no country they could have no passports, and were therefore unable to move from the first country in which they had taken refuge, even if work were waiting for them elsewhere.

Begun at the end of 1922, Dr. Nansen's relief work among refugees was carried on, so far as the very exiguous funds granted by the Assembly permitted, till the end of 1924, when the Council decided to transfer responsibility to the International Labour Organization, on the ground that the problem had by that time become more one of employment than of charitable relief. Dr. Nansen's hands were, however, by no means freed by this arrangement, as the Assembly had just asked him to deal particularly with another refugee problem, that of those Armenians who had found continued existence in Turkey impossible, and had made their way to Greece and other parts of the Balkans.

To turn to the more permanent tasks falling under

the head "humanitarian," mention may be made first of the work of the Opium Advisory Committee. This body is of importance in that after it had been at work for some two years the United States, which is particularly interested in the opium question, decided to send representatives to attend it. There is also a German member on the Commission. The problem hardly needs defining. It consists in concerting international measures by which the abuse of opium and its derivatives can be, if not eliminated altogether, reduced to negligible dimensions. It may be added in parenthesis that all measures applying to opium and its products, like morphia and heroin, apply equally to coca-leaf, and its product, cocaine. Difficulties in the way of effective reform are enormous, for the drugs in question can be so easily smuggled and command such high prices that to keep a hold on the illicit trade is next to impossible. Attempts to deal with the problem were made through a convention signed as a result of a Hague Conference in 1912. The war, however, intervened before the convention could be made really effective, and in point of fact when the League came into existence very few States had ever ratified it. The first business of the League was to press continually for the general ratification of this convention, and secondly to extend and strengthen the terms of the convention. In the former task it was reasonably successful, the value of a permanent secretariat to keep in touch with signatory States and look after what might otherwise have been nobody's business being strikingly demonstrated in this as in many other fields. When it came to improving on the Hague Convention, one step of some importance the League was able to effect was the extension to a large number of States of the import and export certificate system, under which the Government of an exporting country undertakes not to grant licenses for opium or its derivatives to be exported, unless it has received a certificate from the Government of the importing country declaring that this particular consignment is needed for legitimate purposes. So far as this system was adopted, it did provide a real check on traffic for undesirable purposes. It was, however, by no means enough, and the League early adopted a thesis, on which the Americans in particular laid great stress, that what was essential was to limit the world production of these drugs to the amount needed for medical and scientific purposes only. That amount was roughly ascertainable, and it was proposed that every country should send in in advance every year to a Central Board at Geneva an estimate of what it was likely to require for medical and scientific purposes alone in the ensuing twelve months. That would enable the Board to inform the few producing countries of the total amount required and to allocate the demand among them. In such a way there would be no surplus available for illicit trading. These endeavours were complicated by two great obstacles. One, which was ultimately surmounted, was the claim by India to continue to produce opium for internal use, for opium in India is eaten (not smoked) as a kind of homely specific, effective or otherwise, for various diseases. That meant that strictly speaking India would not be limiting production to medical and scientific purposes. Much more serious was the fact that China, which in 1913 had succeeded in abolishing the growth of the opium poppy almost completely, was as a result of her political unsettlement producing again on an enormous scale, though the growth of poppies still remained technically illegal. As a consequence opium was being smuggled out of China in large quantities, and at an International Conference summoned by the League at the end of 1924 it was felt that no satisfactory conclusion could be reached till China had set her own house in order. Consequently an agreement was signed by the States having Far Eastern possessions where opium smoking was still continued, undertaking to abolish the practice finally within fifteen years at most from the date on which an impartial League Commission should declare that the producing countries (primarily China) had so far controlled their production as to remove the danger of smuggling. A second agreement was also signed imposing very severe restrictions on opium smoking, and a third and much more important covention provided for comprehensive international control of the traffic in manufactured drugs. Under this system each nation will estimate in advance its annual needs for purely medical and scientific purposes, and the importation of drugs up to that amount and no more will be authorized by a Central Board established under the auspices of the League at Geneva.

On the same basis as the Opium Advisory Committee stands a similar committee charged with watching the interests of women and children so far as they are affected by international action. For the first five years of the League's existence this meant concentration on means for ensuring the suppression of the so-called white slave traffic—involving the actual seduction and transport of women and girls from one country to another for immoral purposes. To this end a convention was framed in 1921 and approved by the Second Assembly in that year, providing among other things for the general ratification of certain previous conventions on the subject, for the levelling-up by different countries of their legislation bearing on this subject and for the extension, where necessary, of extradition laws affecting it, and for the general adoption of precautions and regulations concerning emigration and immigration calculated to reduce the dangers to which women and children may be exposed in the process.

The work of the Advisory Committee on Women and Children, and of that section of the Secretariat which serves it, consists largely of supervising the working of this convention—no unimportant task in itself, for here as in the case of the prohibition of obscene literature a convention gains a new value now that a permanent central body exists at Geneva to watch the working of the instrument and seek and co-ordinate information regarding it from different countries. The League may indeed convert an international agreement from a dead letter into a living force.

This particular committee, however, has not confined its activities within the limits of the 1921 convention. It has conducted two important inquiries, one into the actual facts of the white slave traffic, a matter on which little adequate information existed, and another into the reasons why different countries have retained or abolished, as the case may be, the system of State regulation, and with what results. In the latter part of 1924 the work of the Advisory Committee (on which the United States is represented) was expanded by the decision of the Assembly that the League should take over an organization known as the Institute for Child Welfare, at that time established at Brussels. It cannot be claimed of the majority of activities coming under the head of child welfare that they are international in character, and the sphere of a League organization working in that field will therefore be rather more circumscribed than might appear. But there is little doubt that it will find useful openings for itself as it develops.

A question which the League, after a good deal of preliminary discussion, has begun to study in earnest is that of slavery, which still exists in various forms in different parts of the world on a larger scale than is commonly suspected. The matter was brought before the Third Assembly in 1922 by Sir Arthur Steel-Maitland, but certain Governments, including the British, showed some reluctance to supply the League with information necessary for its inquiries, with the result that it was not till the latter part of 1924 that a Committee on Slavery was definitely constituted, and not till the Assembly in September of that year that the range of the Committee's investigations was defined. Some question arose on that point, there being a difference of opinion as to whether the Committee should deal merely with the traffic in slaves from one country to another or with all circumstances in which men or women are being compelled to work under conditions other than those of free service. The Committee itself desired wide terms of reference, and it was finally agreed that it should study not simply the slave traffic, but any form of forced labour, together with such transactions as the adoption of children or the acquisition of girls by means of a fictitious dowry or the pledging of human service for debt. The Committee was thus entrusted by the Fifth Assembly with a commission to conduct an inquiry more radical and comprehensive as well as more authoritative than any yet prosecuted into labour conditions in the undeveloped regions of the world.

Reference may conveniently be made here to the League's work in the field of intellectual co-operation, though this falls strictly under the head neither of a technical organization nor of humanitarian activities. The Committee on Intellectual Co-operation was created by a resolution of the Second Assembly in 1921, its object being sufficiently defined in a report presented to the Assembly of the following year in which the Committee was described as existing " to secure for intellectual work the place which befits it and to assist in the freer and more rapid circulation of the great intellectual currents of the world." The Committee numbered among its members such men and women of distinction as Professor Einstein, Professor Henri Bergson, Madame Curie and Professor Gilbert Murray and the well-known American physicist, Dr. Millikan. Some vagueness prevailed as to its precise line of work, but it has gradually developed its own programme, based on the principle that in the field of intellectual pursuits at all events no national frontiers can exist. One effect of the Committee's creation has been the establishment, as part of the Secretariat at Geneva, of a University Information Office designed to provide every kind of information about University courses in different countries and to effect gradually some co-ordination of courses and degrees and the exchange of students and professors. With a view to stimulating the exchange of ideas and experiences national committees in direct touch with the Committee on Intellectual Co-operation have been formed in a number of countries.

The Committee has always been hampered by lack of funds, for the League can only vote it a modest subvention from its budget. Individual countries were, however, encouraged to do what they could to help the Committee, and accordingly in 1924 France offered a building and an annual subsidy of 1,000,000 francs for maintenance, and Italy a building and an annual subsidy of 1,000,000 lire—the former to be used for the general work of the Committee and the latter particularly for the study of the unification of private law. Some natural hesitation was felt at this dispersion by sections of the League working to centres other than Geneva, but in the end the gifts were accepted with appreciation, and from 1925 the Committee on Intellectual Co-operation accordingly carried on its work mainly from Paris and Rome.

CHAPTER XII

THE MANDATE SYSTEM

Article XXII—What the Peace Conference did—A, B, and C
Mandates—The Mandates Commission—Safeguarding
the Native—The Bondelswart Rebellion—Sympathetic
Scrutiny.

THE mandate system embodied in Article XXII of
the Covenant marks a new departure in colonial
administration, and creates a new status in international law. The principle embodied in the Covenant,
at the instance primarily of General Smuts, provided
that certain territories in Africa, Asia and the Pacific,
belonging formerly to the defeated Powers, Germany
and Turkey, should be taken from their former owners,
but neither given their independence nor annexed by
the victors either as colonies or as protectorates.
They were, to put it shortly, to be put something
in the position of a ward in civil law, whose affairs
are administered on his behalf by a trustee till he is
of age to manage them himself. To quote the rather
unexpectedly idealistic language of Article XXII :

" To those colonies and territories which as a consequence
of the late war have ceased to be under the sovereignty of
the States which formerly governed them, and which are
inhabited by peoples not yet able to stand by themselves
under the strenuous conditions of the modern world, there
should be applied the principle that the well-being and development of such peoples form a sacred trust of civilization, and
that securities for the performance of this trust should be
embodied in this Covenant."

It is provided, therefore (in the next paragraph of the Article), that the tutelage of such peoples shall be entrusted to various advanced nations who are willing to accept it, and that this tutelage shall be exercised by them as Mandatories on behalf of the League.

In this matter, as in so many others, the League did not start with free hands, the first steps regarding mandates being taken by the Allied Powers during the Paris Peace Conference in 1919. It was they who divided up the German colonies among different Mandatories, and they too who similarly divided up Turkey's lost possessions in Asia at the San Remo Conference of April 1920. That is how it comes about that none but Allied Powers have been chosen to exercise the function of Mandatory. The League's task consisted in the first instance in approving the terms of the Mandate under which the trust was to be exercised in each case, and from that moment it was with the Council of the League, acting normally through its Permanent Mandates Commission, that the ultimate responsibility for the good administration of mandate territories rested.

Before discussing the Mandates Commission's methods of working, something must be said on the different classes of mandates and the classification of the territories concerned under each of them. There are three categories of mandates, one known as A mandates, applied to territories sufficiently developed to be within measurable distance of independence; one known as C mandates, for territories (like South Africa or the Pacific Islands) best administered as part of the Mandatory's own dominions; and an intermediate class, in some ways the most important, applicable to various African territories, administered independently of any other territory, where specific safeguards for the welfare of the native, like the liquor and arms traffic, are necessary.

In those three categories the mandates are allocated as follows, the name of the Mandatory appearing in brackets in each case :

A. Palestine (Great Britain), Syria and Lebanon (France).
B. Tanganyika (Great Britain), Togoland and Cameroons (divided between Great Britain and France), Ruanda and Urundi (a part of Tanganyika handed over to Belgium under mandate).
C. South-West Africa (Union of South Africa), Pacific Islands north of the Equator (Japan), Samoa (New Zealand), German New Guinea (Australia), Nauru (British Empire).

A special word is called for regarding Iraq. This was always intended to be an A mandate, with Great Britain as mandatory. Before, however, the terms of the mandate had ever been definitely approved by the League Council, it appeared to the British Government that it would be well to contemplate an early grant of independence to Iraq, without the actual issue of a mandate (to which the people of Iraq took some objection) at all. A treaty was accordingly signed between Great Britain and Iraq, embodying all the administrative safeguards which a mandate would have provided, and laid before the League Council for its approval, which was accorded in September 1924.

It was obviously an open question at the outset whether the mandate system was to be merely a disguised, and therefore insincere, form of annexation, or whether it meant establishing real safeguards for the natives. After five years it has been convincingly demonstrated that the system is an effective reality and no pretence. For that credit is due partly to the efficiency and broadmindedness of the Mandates Commission and partly to the value of the opportunities provided for the discussion of any abuses or alleged abuses from the Assembly platform.

Of the two factors the Mandates Commission is the more important. The success of the Commission is largely due to decisions taken at the outset regarding its composition. Its business being to examine reports sent in by Mandatory States on their administration, it was laid down that the Commission should not consist of nominees of Governments, that representatives of States holding mandates should be in a minority, and that no persons in an official position in their own countries should sit. Ex-officials are in another category, their administrative experience often making them valuable members. No one, for example, has done more useful work on the Commission than Sir Frederick Lugard, a former Governor of Nigeria, who was appointed not by the British Government, but, like all members of the Commission, by the League Council.

The procedure under which the mandate system is worked is of some importance. The basis of everything is the individual mandate granted to a particular mandatory in respect of a particular territory—let us say to Great Britain in respect of the area, formerly German East Africa, which is now known as Tanganyika. The mandate for Tanganyika, as approved by the League Council, required the British Government to "promote to the utmost the material and moral well-being and the social progress of its inhabitants," and in particular to abolish slavery and suppress the slave-trade; to prohibit forced labour; to exercise strict control over the arms and liquor traffic; to safeguard the natives' rights in the matter of land transfer; to ensure complete freedom of conscience and worship ; and to keep an open door economically for all members of the League. No military or naval bases may be established in the territory nor any native military force organized for use outside it. Substantially similar provisions are found in all Class B mandates. The A and C class are on a different footing. The former concerns nations approaching the stage of independence, the mandatory's function in this case consisting in giving what is rather vaguely termed " administrative advice and assistance." The latter apply to territories which it is decided for different reasons are best administered as an integral part of the Mandatory's own possessions. Here, however, it is laid down that the Mandatory shall promote to the utmost the material and moral well-being and the social progress of the inhabitants," and the same prohibitions regarding the slave trade and forced labour apply as in B mandates. In the case of the liquor traffic indeed the provisions of the C mandate are the more rigorous, for the supply of alcohol to natives is prohibited altogether. The provisions regarding military and naval bases and military service appear in the C mandates also.

All the mandates having been thus allocated by the Allied and Associated Powers, their precise terms approved by the League Council and the Permanent Mandates Commission being constituted at Geneva, the mandate system might be regarded as in working order. Regarding its procedure the essential features are the rendering by each Mandatory of an annual report for every area entrusted to it under mandate, and the examination of such reports by the Mandates Commission in the presence of a representative of the Mandatory. This is the great safeguard for sound administration, for all the proceedings of the Commission are published, and any shortcomings it may bring to light on the part of a Mandatory are thus exposed to the censure of the world. It is noteworthy indeed that the only criticism directed against the Commission has been on the ground not of its condonation of abuses, but of the severity of certain of its strictures.

The case in point was the discussion that arose in 1922–3 about the methods followed by the Union of South Africa in the suppression of a rebellion of the Bondelswart Hottentots in the mandated area of South-West Africa. Before 1920 the methods South Africa adopted would have been South Africa's business and no one else's. Since 1920, South-West Africa being a mandate area, they were essentially the League's business and in particular the Mandates Commission's. The Commission accordingly conducted the most searching examinations into the facts as disclosed by the Mandatory's report and explained by the representative of the Mandatory who appeared before the Commission, and being by no means satisfied with what they heard, stated frankly in their minutes that they were by no means satisfied. Candid comments on the Bondelswart affair were also made by various speakers from the Assembly platform. South Africa, as has been indicated, felt it was rather unjustly criticized. That may or may not be so. The rights and wrongs of the Bondelswarts operations cannot be discussed here. The incident has been referred to only to show that if the Mandate's Commission errs at all in its conception of its duties it errs in taking them too seriously rather than not seriously enough.

It must not be thought, moreover, that the Commission probes a mandate report thus diligently only when some abuse is suspected. On the contrary, it goes fully each year into the conditions prevailing in each mandate area. The reports are circulated and studied by members of the Commission before they are discussed with the representative of the Mandatory in a formal session, and most of the members have concentrated particularly on some one branch of administration, such as education or health or the liquor traffic or the land tenure system, examining each report, and interrogating each Mandatory's representative, with special reference to administration in this regard in the area in question. Such examination is conducted in a uniformly sympathetic spirit, but it is sufficiently thorough to justify completely the claim that trusteeship under the League is a very real guarantee of the just government of native races. A further safeguard is the provision, of which no great advantage has been taken as yet, that petitions may be addressed to the Mandates Commission by the inhabitants of a mandated area through the Mandatory, who is pledged to forward them at once to Geneva with or without observations of his own on their contents.

CHAPTER XIII

THE SAAR AND DANZIG

The Treaty and the Saar—Inherent Difficulties—The Governing Commission—The Commission and the Council— Danzig as Free Port—Poland's Rights—The League as Arbiter.

THE League in different ways is responsible for the good government of the area between Lorraine and Germany known as the Saar Valley, and the free city of Danzig on the Baltic, at the mouth of the River Vistula. Neither task is of the League's own seeking. Both were imposed on it by the Treaty of Versailles before the League itself was in existence at all, and both came to it hedged about with such Treaty conditions and provisos that the best that could be hoped for was to escape absolute failure, without any possibility of attaining real success.

That is particularly true of the Saar. This important industrial area is of about 700 square miles in area and contains a population of roughly 700,000. Before the war three systems of administration affected it, for part of the territory was under Prussia and part under Bavaria and all, of course, subject to the general laws of the German Empire. Its mines were given to France under the Treaty. With their administration the League has nothing to do. The area was also to come (and has come) into the French customs system in 1925. The Treaty provided for a new administration under a Governing Commission of five members, appointed by the League Council. It was to be quite arbitrary in character, for though the Commission was to include one French member and one inhabitant of the Saar, as well as three who were neither French nor German, the Saar member was to be appointed like the rest, by the League Council, and was in no sense a representative of the inhabitants, whose views on the subject need not be, and in point of fact have not been, ascertained. Though the Council appoints the Commissioners year by year, and can, if necessary, cancel their appointments, it has no direct control over the Saar. The Commission itself is the instrument of government.

That does not exhaust the difficulties of the situation. According to the Treaty, Saar inhabitants are to decide by a free vote in 1935 between the three alternatives of full reunion with Germany, transference to France and continuance of the League régime. There is little doubt, of course, that they will choose the first, and no possibility of their choosing the second. It is conceivable, however, that they might in the end be tempted to decide for a continuance of the present system, under which they bear no share in the payment of German reparations. That being so, it is necessary for every patriotic German in the Saar and out of it to do everything to discredit the Governing Commission in the eyes of the inhabitants, and it carries on its work in an atmosphere of unabated hostility and suspicion.

The greatest danger the League had to face in the Saar was of seeming to act not as a completely impartial agent, holding a studiously even balance between France and Germany, but as something like an instrument of the victorious Powers. It cannot be pretended that that danger has been altogether avoided. The Governing Commission, as originally constituted by the League Council, consisted, as the Treaty prescribed, of one French member and one Saarois, together with a Canadian, a Belgian and a Dane. Of these the Belgian and the French naturally stood together, and the Dane, though nominally citizen of a neutral country, was in fact a man whose French sympathies, based on an almost life-long residence in Paris, were notorious. There was always, therefore, in case of need a French majority of three out of five on the Commission. The French member, moreover, was in 1920 appointed the first President of the Commission, and his mandate was renewed in 1921, 1922, 1923 and 1924. In the course of those years the Canadian member was succeeded by another Canadian, the Dane first by a Spaniard and then (on his death) by a Czechoslovakian, while the occupant of the Saar chair had been changed three times. The original French and Belgian members remained.

All things considered, the Commission has done its administrative work well, and though critics of the régime have been given plenty of material for their attacks (mainly as a result of the provisions of the Treaty of Versailles, by which the hands of the Commission were tied), there were few, if any, grievances of real substance. The rights of the inhabitants in such matters as education and religion have been fully maintained, and the existing legal system has been preserved. The district is prosperous, and apart from political grievances, usually studiously exaggerated, has little ground for discontent. A consultative council of the inhabitants has been created, but it has no power to do anything beyond laying its views before the Governing Commission. The right of criticism divested of responsibility is rarely beneficial, and it is not surprising that Council and Commission are in frequent opposition.

It is to be regretted that the League was not given the Saar Valley to run in its own way. With a free hand it would almost certainly have succeeded a good deal better than it has been able to when fettered by the Treaty. Even so, Commission government under the League has been shown to be a perfectly practical proposition, which might be adopted with advantage in other areas where an international régime may prove desirable.

The status of Danzig differs materially from that of the Saar. The area is roughly the same and the population (350,000) about half, but while the Saar is controlled absolutely by its Governing Commission Danzig is a Free City with its own Senate and Chamber, but with a League High Commissioner to hold the balance between it and its neighbour Poland. The peculiar relationship of Danzig to Poland is the source of all the League's troubles concerning it. Till the war Danzig was one of the great ports of Germany, holding a commanding position at the mouth of the River Vistula, down which all the trade of the now Polish hinterland passed. When the three divided sections of Poland—Russian, Austrian and German— were reunited, the new State was given access to the sea by a narrow " corridor " running down the Vistula valley. Normally the corridor might have been expected to include Danzig, and the Poles were bitterly disappointed that the Peace Conference decided otherwise. But Danzig is German through and through, and it was felt that to hand it over to Polish sovereignty would be unjustifiable. On the other hand, the claims of Poland to the free use of the port—all of whose commercial connections were with the Polish hinterland—were strong and the expedient was, therefore, devised of severing the city from Germany without uniting it to Poland. It governs itself, as it did a century and more ago, and Poland is given various rights in such matters as railways, customs and the use of the port. In addition to the provisions on these questions in the Treaty of Versailles a separate treaty between Danzig and Poland was drafted and signed in 1920, designed to provide for any contingency likely to arise. The rôle of the High Commissioner is to give an impartial ruling in the name of the League on any matter in dispute between Poland, which has a permanent diplomatic representative in Danzig, and the Free City. From such rulings an appeal lies to the League Council. At first both Danzig and Poland regularly appealed on principle against every decision given, with the result that the League Council was flooded with a number of trivial questions that ought never to have come to it. Gradually, however, the habit of settlement by direct agreement, through the mediation of the High Commissioner or officials of the League Secretariat at Geneva, developed and only major disputes reached the League Council table. In 1923–4 the Danzig currency was reformed and put on a sound basis in accordance with a plan prepared by the League's Financial and Economic Organization.

The Danzig scheme, like the Saar régime, is an interesting experiment from which lessons can be derived that might be applicable elsewhere. In both cases the League has been called on to facilitate the working of a plan drawn up without its concurrence and so framed as to make real success unattainable. There are no two sets of questions which, in proportion to their magnitude, cause the Secretariat more anxiety. That the results of five years' working have been satisfactory it would be foolish to claim. What it is fair to say is that though failure under conditions so difficult would have been no discredit to the League, it has in point of fact neither failed nor come near failing.

CHAPTER XIV

THE LEAGUE AND MINORITIES

The Minority Treaties—Voluntary Undertakings—Rights of Minorities—League Methods—Mediation and Legal Rulings—A Minorities Commission ?

THE responsibility for the protection of Minorities in Europe was laid on the League by a series of treaties between the Allied and Associated Powers and various European States in 1919 and 1920. There is not a word regarding Minorities in the Covenant, and the League as a League was never consulted before this important task was assigned to it. Most of the States of Continental Europe have always included within their borders a certain number of persons whose race, religion or language, or all three, differed from, that of the State in which they lived. The Peace Settlement of 1919, with its extensive rearrangement of political frontiers, created new Minority problems throughout Central Europe and many of them became the more acute in that a race which had been dominant, and as such had acted with severity towards the Minority within its borders, became in its turn a Minority subject to the sovereignty of the very race over which it had hitherto tyrannized. The bottom dog, in fact, had become the top dog. Transylvania, where Rumanians were formerly under Hungarian sovereignty, and Hungarians are now under Rumania, is an obvious example. In point of fact it is difficult to compute the number of such racial Minorities in Europe, but they total certainly not less, and probably much more, than 30,000,000. Their existence is inevitable, but the discontent to which unjust treatment of Minorities may give rise is a potent cause of war. Austria's fear and suspicion of certain of the Minorities within her borders was one of the prime causes of the outbreak in 1914. The League's task therefore in guaranteeing, or attempting to guarantee, fair treatment for all Minorities is neither light nor unimportant. Its authority is derived from some ten Treaties under which the States possessing large Minority populations gave undertakings to the Allied Powers regarding the treatment of such Minorities, the League being nominated in each Treaty as the final arbiter. In addition a number of States, notably Esthonia, Latvia, Lithuania and Albania, were persuaded on entering the League to accept voluntarily similar obligations to those imposed on the other States by Treaty. These obligations were substantially the same in each case and can be sufficiently indicated by one or two quotations from the first treaty signed at Paris in 1919, between the Allied Powers and Poland.

Under Article II of this treaty it is laid down that " all inhabitants of Poland shall be entitled to the free exercise whether public or private of any creed, religion or belief whose practices are not inconsistent with public order or public morals." Other articles provide that all Polish nationals, without distinction of race, language or religion, shall enjoy the same civil and political privileges, that the Minorities shall have the right to maintain their own schools and other institutions, and that in districts where Minorities form a considerable portion of the population, instruction in the State schools shall be given in the language of the Minority. The vital clause in all the Minority Treaties is that under which it is laid down that the undertakings regarding Minorities " constitute an obligation of international concern and shall be placed under the guarantee of the League of Nations." What this means is that whereas under normal circumstances interference by an outside power in the interests of a Minority would be a distinctly unfriendly act and might easily precipitate war (as indeed it has done in many recent cases in history), it now becomes the acknowledged and unquestionable right of the League to intervene when circumstances seem to require it.

How, in point of fact, is the League discharging its obligations ? Its organization for dealing with Minority problems consists of a special section of the League Secretariat, together with a sub-committee of the Council, consisting of the President for the time being and any other two members he may name. When complaints are received by or on behalf of a Minority they are first considered by the Secretariat. It is laid down, moreover, that they must be communicated at once to the State of which the Minority forms part, and in many cases the matter can be put right at once, particularly when the friendly offices of members of the Secretariat are available. Abuses are constantly due to the arbitrary administration by some official in a province distant from the capital, and the central government is commonly ready to intervene when its attention is called to the trouble by private representations from Geneva. At the same time there may of course be more serious grievances, which yield to mediation less readily. In these cases it is laid down that any member of the

Council may raise the matter, the only reason for the existence of a sub-committee of three being to ensure that any grievance which ought to be considered is not overlooked. In point of fact, not many complaints have been dealt with by the Council itself. Two which did come before it, both of them concerning German Minorities in Poland, raised legal questions which were referred by the Council to the Permanent Court of International Justice. The Court found in each case in favour of Germany, and the Council then set itself successfully to carry through an agreement on the basis of the Court's rulings.

It cannot be claimed that the protection of Minorities is by any means completely effective, nor is it easy to see how it could be. The circumstances are always difficult, with rights and wrongs on one side as well as the other. Minorities are just as often unreasonable as the dominant State is arbitrary in its treatment, and the League accordingly has as often to restrain the one party as to remonstrate with the other. Minority problems, moreover, go to the root of national sovereignty, a matter on which every State is abnormally sensitive, particularly States whose histories are short and whose political position none too secure. That has so far prevented the League from developing certain machinery whose creation would undoubtedly be of value. In Upper Silesia, under the terms of the National Polish Agreement of 1922, a Minority office to deal with complaints has been set up on each side of the frontier, with very successful results. To create similar institutions elsewhere would be most desirable. The question of appointing League Commissioners, to reside in areas where Minority difficulties are known to be particularly acute, was fully discussed at the Third Assembly, and an agreement to try the experiment almost reached. Certain States, however, objected, and the unanimity necessary for the adoption of the project could not be obtained. The value of such resident commissioners has been illustrated by the recourse voluntarily had by Greece and Bulgaria, in connection with certain difficult questions on their Macedonian frontier, to the good offices of a League Commission which happened to be working on that frontier in connection with another matter. Arising out of that, the Greek and Bulgarian representatives at the Fifth Assembly each signed a voluntary agreement with the League Council to refer Minority questions regularly to the same Commission. Bulgaria duly ratified the agreement, but Greece for various political reasons unfortunately declined to do so.

It is sometimes assumed that all Minorities have the right to appeal to the League. That is by no means the case. The League's authority is derived only from the particular Treaties under which the Minority question is dealt with. No such treaty protects, for example, the Austrians of the Southern Tyrol now under Italian sovereignty. Comparison may not unjustly be made between the League machinery in the case of mandates, and in that of Minorities. The former is very largely successful because of the existence of a standing Mandates Commission, to which reports on mandate administration are annually rendered and which can discuss any difficulties or abuses in the unsensational atmosphere of a committee room. The Mandates Commission moreover, partly by its original composition and partly by the experience it has gathered in working, has made itself thoroughly experienced in mandate questions. The creation of a Minorities Commission, carefully selected and subject of course on all points to the League Council, on similar lines, could hardly fail to be of great value. No constitutional difficulties stand in the way of the creation of such a Commission, and it seems not impossible that its formation may be the next step in the development of more effective machinery for dealing with Minority questions.

CHAPTER XV

AFTER FIVE YEARS

Gaps to be filled—Actual Achievements—The " Geneva Atmosphere "—Small Tasks or Great ?

AT the end of five years the League of Nations was still incomplete. Three great States—Germany, Russia and the United States—were not members of it, though Germany in the latter part of 1924 took certain definite steps which appeared to point to an application for membership from her at the Assembly of 1925. In addition Egypt, Mexico, Afghanistan and Turkey were not members of the League. Apart from that, it included every State of importance in the civilized world. On the foundations laid by the Covenant it had built up comprehensive and efficient machinery for dealing with any task referred to it under its original constitution, or likely to devolve on it from other sources. It had in particular created the Permanent Court of International Justice, which introduced a new element of authority into legal relationships between nations.

The Assembly, through its arrangements for regular annual meetings, and still more through the special character imparted to it by the fact that its members meet pledged to uphold the ideals unequivocally set forth in the Covenant, has generated a cohesiveness and a disposition to make any reasonable sacrifices in the interests of constructive agreement which distinguishes it markedly from other international conferences of which the world has had recent experience. The Council, meeting at more frequent intervals, and with a proportionately larger share of responsibility falling on each of its ten members, has developed a certain *esprit de corps* which tends to make it a matter of honour to carry through to success any task undertaken. Yet it is in some ways to the third and subsidiary organ of the League, the Secretariat, that the whole Society so far owes most, for it is the Secretariat which gives the League that element of permanence and continuity which enables it to apply itself tirelessly and without intermission to a particular problem till the solution is finally reached. The Council may meet for only some ten days at a time, but when it reassembles three months later it can take up its business again exactly where it was left, or rather with all the advantage of inquiries pursued and information acquired by the Secretariat in the intervening period. It is the Secretariat which, without ever initiating policy, for that lies entirely beyond its sphere, maintains contacts permanently with all members of the League, obtains and sets in order the facts on which the Assembly or Council or special committees must act, and informs itself continually of the way in which decisions by any of these parties are being executed.

Much is heard, particularly from speakers and writers with personal experience of Geneva, of the unique international " atmosphere " prevailing there. Such an atmosphere unquestionably exists, and there are those who view it with some misgiving as tending to impel delegates in a moment of enthusiasm to decisions or agreements which their Governments at home might subsequently decline to ratify. Such cases have occurred sufficiently often to prove that the criticism is not unjustified. The tendency, none the less, must be looked on as a defect attendant (though it may be hoped not inevitably attendant) on a quality the existence of which is to be welcomed. The League has beyond any doubt created new standards in international relationships. The ideal of international co-operation embodied in the opening words of the Preamble of the Covenant has been realized to a degree that may astonish not merely cynics but optimists. States do actually send their delegates, and increasingly responsible delegates (there were at the Fifth Assembly seven Premiers and sixteen Foreign Ministers), to co-operate internationally by any means possible rather than to seek merely the advantage of the country they represent. Too much may no doubt be made of this characteristic of League gatherings as distinguished from other international conferences. The difference, it may be conceded, is one merely of degree. It exists none the less, and it provides the best possible demonstration that the League in five years of practical work has not failed to realize the first ideals of its founders. Its future rests in the hands of the States that compose it. That is of course a commonplace, but commonplaces sometimes need repeating, and in this case it is too little realized by those citizens of every country from whom, under any democratic constitution, the Government of the country must in the last resort take its mandate, that even machinery as efficient as the League has created may be comparatively valueless if the Governments are not prepared to make full use of it.

At the end of five years the tendency is still plainly visible, on the part particularly of the Greater Powers (the lesser States see in the Covenant their main charter of security), to regard the League as a useful clearing-house for the discussion of secondary questions, and to rely on direct diplomatic interchanges or conversations between groups of interested States for the settlement of those problems which most directly affect their country's destiny. The League was intended to concentrate the strength, the experience, and the conscience of the world in one comprehensive society, of which all States would be members and under which the interest of no single State or group of States would be dominant. It was to be impartial because it would be universal, and so long as it fails to be universal it cannot wholly fulfil its destiny. But still less can it fulfil it unless those States already members of the Society show that in all things they are ready to give it their full confidence.

INDEX

PRINTED BY UNWIN BROTHERS, LIMITED, LONDON AND WOKING, GREAT BRITAIN

For Product Safety Concerns and Information please contact our EU
representative GPSR@taylorandfrancis.com
Taylor & Francis Verlag GmbH, Kaufingerstraße 24, 80331 München, Germany

www.ingramcontent.com/pod-product-compliance
Lightning Source LLC
Chambersburg PA
CBHW071135280326
41935CB00010B/1230